Guiding Those Left Behind

ALL THE LEGAL AND PRACTICAL THINGS
YOU NEED TO DO
TO SETTLE AN ESTATE IN NORTH CAROLINA
and
HOW TO ARRANGE YOUR OWN AFFAIRS
TO AVOID UNNECESSARY COST
TO YOUR FAMILY

By AMELIA E. POHL, ESQ.
with North Carolina attorney
GORDON W. JENKINS
and
BARBARA J. SIMMONDS, Ph.D.
as consulting psychologist

 EAGLE PUBLISHING COMPANY OF BOCA

The purpose of this book is to provide the reader with an accurate and informative overview of the subject but laws change frequently and are subject to different interpretations as courts rule on the meaning or effect of a law. This book is sold with the understanding that neither the publisher nor the authors are engaging in, nor rendering legal, medical, psychiatric, accounting or any other professional service. If you need legal, accounting, medical, psychiatric or other expert advice, then you should seek the services of a duly licensed professional.

WEB SITES: Web sites appear throughout the book. These Web sites are offered for the convenience of the reader only. Publication of these Web site addresses is not an endorsement by the authors, editors or publishers of this book.

This book is intended for use by the consumer for his or her own benefit. If you use this book to counsel someone about the law, accounting or medicine, then that may be considered an unauthorized and illegal practice.

EAGLE PUBLISHING COMPANY OF BOCA
4199 N. Dixie Highway, #2
Boca Raton, FL   33431
E-mail   info@eaglepublishing.com

Printed in the United States of America
ISBN 1-892407-21-3
Library of Congress Card Catalog Number: 00-190356

The Organization of the Book

If you are going to GUIDE THOSE LEFT BEHIND, you need to know what is involved in settling an estate in North Carolina, so we begin the book explaining that process. The first six chapters explain:

1. How to tend to the funeral and burial
2. What agencies need to be notified of the death
3. How to locate the decedent's property
4. What bills need (and do not need) to be paid.
5. Determining who are the beneficiaries
6. Getting the decedent's property to the proper beneficiary

We devoted a chapter to each of these 6 steps; and for those who are in the process of settling an estate, we placed a CHECK LIST at the end of Chapter 6 to assist in remembering things that need to be done.

Once you read Chapters 1 through 6 you will be able to identify those problems that can occur when someone dies. Using those Chapters as a base, chapters 7 and 8 explain how to set up your own estate plan so that your family is not burdened by similar problems. Chapter 9 offers suggestions that you may find helpful if you or a member of your family are having difficulty getting through the grieving process.

GLOSSARY

This book is designed for the average reader. Legal terminology has been kept to a minimum. There is a glossary at the end of the book in the event you come across a legal term that is not familiar to you.

FICTITIOUS NAMES AND EVENTS

The examples in this book are based loosely on actual events; however, all names are fictitious; and the events, as portrayed, are fictitious.

The Consulting Psychologist

BARBARA J. SIMMONDS, Ph.D., a noted psychologist, has collaborated with the author on the last chapter of this book dealing with the grieving process. Dr. Simmonds has been practicing in the field of Health/Rehabilitation Psychology and Gerontology for the past 10 years. Her experiences in the field led her as a natural outcome to develop expertise also in Grief Counseling, since so many losses accrue to individuals in a health care setting.

In addition to her work in hospitals, nursing centers and private practice, Dr. Simmonds has served as Adjunct Faculty at Nova Southeastern University, teaching courses in Aging, Stress Management and Grief Counseling. Dr. Simmonds holds a Master's Degree in Gerontology and a Ph.D. in Clinical Psychology from Nova Southeastern University. She was the Director of Psychological Services at Villa Maria Nursing and Rehabilitation Center for eight years and now continues her relationship with the institution on a consultation basis. She continues with her private practice in North Miami, Florida

About the Author

Before becoming an attorney in 1985, AMELIA E. POHL taught mathematics on both the high school and college level. During her tenure as Associate Professor of Mathematics at Prince George's Community College in Maryland, she wrote several books including Probability: A Set Theory Approach, Principals of Counting and Common Stock Sense.

During her practice of law Attorney Pohl observed that many people want to reduce the high cost of legal fees by performing or assisting with their own legal transactions. Attorney Pohl found that, with a bit of guidance, people are able to perform many legal transactions for themselves. Attorney Pohl utilizes her background as teacher, author and attorney to provide that "bit of guidance" to the general public in the form of self-help legal books that she has written. Attorney Pohl is currently "translating" this book for the remaining 49 states:

Guiding Those Left Behind In Alabama,
Guiding Those Left Behind In Connecticut, etc.

Consulting North Carolina Attorney

GORDON W. JENKINS has practiced law in Winston-Salem since graduating from the University of North Carolina in 1974. Prior to law school, he attended Duke University, graduating in 1968 with a BA degree. He served in the US Army from September 1969 until being honorably discharged as a 1st Lieutenant in April, 1972.

Licensed to practice law in North Carolina and in the Federal District Court for the Middle District of North Carolina, Mr. Jenkins is a senior partner in an eight person firm, Wells Jenkins Lucas & Jenkins, PLLC. Mr. Jenkins has concentrated his practice in the area of Estate Planning and Administration during the last decade. He is Board Certified in Estate Planning and Probate Law by the North Carolina State Bar.

Gordon W. Jenkins has been active in the local and state legal community, having served as President of the Forsyth County Bar Association; President of the Board of Directors, Legal Aid Society of Northwest North Carolina; and president of the Estate Planning Council of Winston-Salem. In addition, he is a member of the Wake Forest University Planned Giving Council, the North Carolina Bar Association Foundation Development Committee and the North Carolina Bar Association Elder Law Section Council.

A native of Winston-Salem, Mr. Jenkins is active in his church, First Presbyterian, where he has served as both a deacon and an elder. In recent years he has participated in Leadership Winston-Salem, been appointed to the Forsyth County Library Board of Trustees, and been a member of the Board of Directors of Associates in Christian counseling.

Mr. Jenkins is married and has two children.

To my brother, Paul Adinolfi,
his intelligence, good humor and kindness,
his strength during our times of family loss,
have set the beacon standard for me to follow.

ACKNOWLEDGMENT

When someone dies, the family attorney is often among the first to be called. Family members have questions about whether probate is necessary, who to notify, how to get possession of the assets, etc. Over the years, as we practiced in the field of Elder Law, we noticed that the questions raised were much the same family to family. We both agreed that a book answering such questions would be of service to the general public. We wish to thank all of the clients, whom we have had the honor and pleasure to serve, for providing us with the impetus to produce this book.

Guiding Those Left Behind

CONTENTS

About The Book

We tried to make this book as comprehensive as possible so there are specialized sections of the book that do not apply to the general population and may not be of interest to you. The following GUIDE POSTS appear throughout the book. You can read the section if the situation applies to you or skip the section if it doesn't.

GUIDE POSTS

The SPOUSE POST means that the information provided is specifically for the spouse of the decedent. If the decedent was single, then skip this section.

The CALL-A-LAWYER POST alerts you to a situation that may require the assistance of an attorney. See page xiii for information about how to find a lawyer.

The CAUTION POST alerts you to a potential problem. It is followed by a suggestion about how to avoid the problem.

The SPECIAL SITUATION POST means that the information given in that paragraph applies to a particular event or situation; for example when the decedent dies a violent death. If the situation does not apply in your case then you can skip the section.

Reading the Law

Where applicable, we identified the state statute or federal statute that is the basis of the discussion. We did this as a reference, and also to encourage the general public to read the law as it is written. Prior to the Internet the only way you could look up the law was to physically take yourself to the local courthouse law library or the law section of a public library. Today all of the state and federal statutes are literally at your finger tips. They are just a mouse click away on the Internet. All you need to look up the law is the address of the Web site and the identifying number of the statute:

 NORTH CAROLINA STATUTE WEB SITE
http://www.ncga.state.nc.us/

FEDERAL STATUTE WEB SITE
http://www4.law.cornell.edu/uscode

North Carolina divides its laws into Chapters. When we refer to North Carolina law we will refer to the chapter and section. For example (NCGS 28B-2) refers to the North Carolina General Statutes, Chapter 28B, Section 2.

If you come across a topic that is of importance to you, then you may find it both interesting and profitable to actually read the law as written.

When You Need A Lawyer

This book describes North Carolina law in effect when the book was written. We pay our legislators (state and federal) to make laws and, if necessary, change those in effect. We pay judges to interpret the law and that interpretation may change the way the law operates. The legislature and the judiciary do their job and so laws change frequently.

The purpose of the book is to give the reader an overview of what needs to be done when someone dies, and to provide information about how a person can arrange his own affairs to avoid problems for his own family. It is not intended as a substitute for legal counsel or any other kind of professional advice. If you have any legal question, then you should to seek the counsel of an attorney. When looking for an attorney, consider three things:
EXPERTISE, COST and PERSONALITY.

EXPERTISE

North Carolina Bar has certification programs for many different areas of law including Bankruptcy, Criminal Law, Immigration, Real Property, Family Law, Estate Planning and Probate. To become Board Certified in any of these areas, the attorney must be experienced in that field of law and must pass an examination.

Certification is just one of the criteria to consider. Many fine attorneys are experienced in an area of law, but have not taken the time, effort and expense to become certified as a specialist by the North Carolina Bar. If the attorney is not certified in the branch of law that you seek, then ask how long he has practiced that type of law and what percentage of his practice is devoted to that branch of law.

Before employing an attorney for a job, ask how long he has practiced that type of law and what percentage of his practice is devoted to that type of law. Ask whether the attorney has any special training or special degrees in the field of law that you seek.

STATE BAR REFERRAL SERVICE

You can call your local county North Carolina Bar for information about how to reach an attorney, in your county, who is experienced in the area of law that you seek. You can also call the North Carolina Bar Association. They have a statewide referral service. Their in state telephone number is (800) 662-7660. For out of state, call (919) 677-8574.

Of course, the best way to find an attorney is through personal referral. Ask your friends, family or business acquaintances if they have used an attorney for the field of law that you seek and whether they were pleased with the results. It is important to employ an attorney who is experienced in the kind of law you seek. Your friend may have a great Estate Planning attorney, but if you have suffered an injury, then you need an attorney who is experienced in Personal Injury.

COST

In addition to the attorney's experience, it is important to check out what to expect to pay in attorney's fees. When you call for an appointment ask what the attorney will charge for the initial consultation and the approximate cost for the service you seek. Ask whether there will be any additional costs such as filing fees, accounting fees, expert witness fees, etc.

If the least expensive attorney is out of your price range then there are many state and private agencies throughout the state that provide legal assistance for people of low income. You can look up the nearest Legal Service Program in your telephone book, or you can call the **LEGAL SERVICES PROGRAM OF NORTH CAROLINA** at their central office in Raleigh (919) 856-2180.

The American Bar Association has a directory of North Carolina Pro Bono Programs at its Web Site:

AMERICAN BAR ASSOCIATION WEB SITE
www.abanet.org/legalservices/probono/pb-North Carolina

PERSONALITY

Of equal importance to the attorney's experience and legal fees, is your relationship with the attorney. How easy was it to reach the attorney? Did you go through layers of receptionists and legal assistants before being allowed to speak to the attorney? Did the attorney promptly return your call? If you had difficulty reaching the attorney, then you can expect similar problems should you employ that attorney.

Did the attorney treat you with respect? Did the attorney treat you paternally with a "father knows best" attitude or did the attorney treat you as an intelligent person with the ability to understand the options available to you and the ability to make your own decision based on the information provided to you. Are you able to understand and easily communicate with the attorney? Is he/she speaking to you in plain English or is his/her explanation of the matter so full of legalese to be almost meaningless to you?

Do you find the attorney's personality to be pleasant or grating? Sometimes people rub each other the wrong way. It is like rubbing a cat the wrong way. Stroking a cat from head to tail is pleasing to the cat, but petting it in the opposite direction, no matter how well intended, causes friction. If the lawyer makes you feel annoyed or uncomfortable, then find another attorney.

It is worth the effort to take the time to interview as many attorneys as it takes to find one with the right expertise, fee schedule and personality for you.

The First Week

1

Dealing with the death of a close family member or friend is difficult. Not only do you need to deal with your own emotions, but often with those of your family and friends. Sometimes their sorrow is more painful to you, than what you are experiencing yourself.

In addition to the emotional impact of a death, there are many things that need to be done, from arranging the funeral and burial, to closing out the business affairs of the decedent, and finally giving whatever property is left to the proper beneficiary.

The funeral and burial take only a few days. Wrapping up the affairs of the *decedent* (the person who died) may take considerably longer. This chapter explains what things you (the spouse or closest family member) need to do during the first week, beginning at the moment of death and continuing through the funeral.

   MALE GENDER USED

Rather than use "he/she" or "his/her" for simplicity
(and hoping not to offend anyone)
we will refer to the decedent and his
Personal Representative using the male gender.

References to other people will be in both genders.

AUTOPSIES

In today's high tech world of medicine, doctors are fairly certain of the cause of death, but if there is a question, the family should consider having an autopsy performed. North Carolina statute 130A-398(6) sets the following order of priority for who may authorize the autopsy:

1. spouse
2. adult child or stepchild
3. parent or stepparent
4. any adult sibling
5. the court appointed guardian of the decedent (if any)
6. a relative who agrees to dispose of the body
7. anyone who is obliged to dispose of the body

If any member of the same or prior class objects, then no autopsy can be performed.

The cost of an autopsy runs anywhere from several hundred to over three thousand dollars. The person giving authorization must agree to pay for the autopsy because the cost is not covered under most health insurance plans. It is in the family's best interest to consent to the autopsy. The examination might reveal a genetic disorder that could be treated if it later appears in another family member. The family member may have died because of incorrect medical treatment or perhaps foul play.

Even if none of these are found, knowing the cause of death with certainty is better than not knowing. That was the case with the family of a woman who was taken to the hospital complaining of stomach pains. The doctors thought she might be suffering from gallbladder disease but she died before they could effectively treat her. A doctor suggested that an autopsy be performed to determine the actual cause of death. The woman had three daughters, one of whom objected to the autopsy:

"Why spend that kind of money?
It won't bring Mom back."

The daughter's wishes were respected and no autopsy was performed. However, over the years, as each of the daughters aged and became ill with their own various ailments they would undergo physical examinations. As part of taking their medical history, doctors would routinely ask "And what was cause of your mother's death?" None could answer the question.

This is not a dramatic story. No mysterious genetic disorder ever occurred in any of her daughters, nor in any of their children. But each daughter (including the one who objected) at some point in her life, was confronted with the nagging question "What did Mom die of?"

MANDATORY AUTOPSIES

When a person dies, a physician must sign the death certificate stating the cause of death. If a person dies in a hospital, then there is a doctor present to sign the certificate. If a person dies at home then the police must be notified. The person who discovers the body should call 911. The police will have the medical examiner determine the cause of death. If the death was not from natural causes, or from a disease that might pose a threat to the public health, then the medical examiner, or the district attorney or any Superior Court judge can order an autopsy to be performed. If performed, the autopsy is paid for by the county where body is found (NCGS 130A-389).

AUTOPSIES PERFORMED BY THE INSURANCE COMPANY:

A company that issues an accident or health insurance policy in North Carolina is required to include a statement in the policy that the company has the right to perform an autopsy. The cost of the autopsy is paid for by the insurance company, so they will not order an autopsy unless there is some important reason to do so (NCGS 58-51-15 (a)(10)).

ANATOMICAL GIFTS

If, before death, the decedent made an anatomical gift by signing a donor card, then hospital personnel or the donor's doctor needs to be made aware of the gift in quick proximity to the time of death — preferably before death.

GIFT AUTHORIZED BY THE FAMILY

Hospital personnel determine whether a mortally ill patient is a candidate for an organ donation. Early on in the donor program those over 65 were not considered as suitable candidates. Today, however, the condition of the organ, and not the age, is the determining factor.

The federal government has established regional Organ Procurement Organizations throughout the United States, to coordinate the donor program. There are Organ Procurement Organizations in Winston Salem (Carolina Lifecare Medical Center), Charlotte (LifeShare of the Carolinas) and Greenville (Carolina Organ Procurement Agency). If it is decided that the patient is a candidate, the hospital will contact the local Organ Procurement Organization.

The Organ Procurement Organization will determine whether the patient is a suitable donor. If they decide to request the gift and the candidate did not sign a donor card then someone in the family must give written permission. Someone who is specially trained will approach the family to request the donation. North Carolina statute 130A-404 establishes an order of priority to authorize the donation:

1st   The spouse
2nd   An adult child
3rd   Either parent
4th   An adult sibling
5th   A court appointed guardian
6th   Anyone authorized to dispose of the body

If permission is obtained from a family member and there are others in the same or a higher priority, then an effort must be made to contact those people and make them aware of the proposed gift. For example, if the sister of the decedent agrees to the gift (4th in priority) and the decedent had an adult child (2nd in priority), then the child needs to be made aware of the gift. If the child objects, then no gift can be made. Similarly, the statute prohibits the gift if the decedent ever expressed his opposition to a donation.

AFTER THE DONATION

If the family agrees to the donation, then once the operation is complete the body is delivered to the funeral home and prepared for burial or cremation as directed by the family. The operation does not disfigure the body so there can be an open casket viewing if the family so wishes.

Once the donation is made, the Organ Procurement Organization keeps in touch with the donor's family. If the family wishes they will provide them with basic demographic information about the donation, such as the age, sex, marital status, number of children and occupation of the recipient of the gift.

If the recipient of the gift wishes to write to the donor's family to thank them for the gift, the Organ Procurement Organization will contact the donor's family and ask if they wish to receive the letter. If not, then the letter is kept on file in the event that the donor's family may want to read it at a later date.

GIFT FOR EDUCATION OR RESEARCH

If the decedent signed a donor card indicating his wish to use his body for any purpose and he is not a candidate for an organ donation, then you can offer to release the body to any of the following institutions to be used for education or research:

Wake Forest University School of Medicine   (336) 716-4369
Department of Neurobilogy and Anatomy
Winston-Salem, NC   27157

Duke University Medical Center   (919) 684-4124
Biological Anthropology and Anatomy
Box 3170
Durham, NC 27710

East Carolina University School of Medicine   (252) 816-2849
Anatomy and Cell Biology Department
Greenville, NC   27834-4354

University of North Carolina   (919) 966-1134
Medical Science Teaching Laboratories
Berryhill Hall, 21911, CB 77520
Chapel Hill, NC   27599

You need to call the school to determine whether they will accept the body. Most schools will not accept bodies from those who are obese or who have died from a contagious disease or from crushing injuries. If the donation is accepted, you will need to pay for the transportation of the body to the school.

The study takes from 18 months to two years to complete. Once the study is complete the remains are cremated and the ashes returned to the family, or if the family wishes the school will have the *cremains* (cremated remains) buried in a local cemetery.

CAVEAT: It is illegal for anyone to purchase body parts. It is legal to charge monies to prepare or transport bodies or body parts. Not-for profit and as well as for-profit companies have sprung up that are in the business of preparing and delivering body parts. These companies request donations from families (so they are not buying body parts). The company prepares the body tissue or other parts of the body, and then distributes the parts throughout the United States to physicians, hospitals, research centers, etc. In many cases the monies charged for preparation and transportation includes a sizable profit. If someone other than your local Organ Procurement Organization (as identified on page 4) approaches you to make a donation, then before making the donation you may want to:

LEARN ABOUT THE COMPANY
You may want to learn about the company requesting the donation:
>What is the name of the company?
>Where are their main headquarters located?
>What is their primary business activity?
>What is the name and job description of the
>person making the request?

DETERMINE THE END USE OF THE DONATION
You may want to ask what they intend to do with the tissue or body part. If it is being used for research, then what type of research? Where is the research being conducted? If it will be used for transplantation, then what agency (doctor, hospital) will receive the donation and where is that agency located?

THE FUNERAL

Approximately ten percent of all deaths occur suddenly because of an accident, suicide, foul play or undetected illness. But most deaths are anticipated with the common scenario being that of a person dying after being ill for many months. Expected or not, the first job is the disposition of the body.

THE PREARRANGED FUNERAL

Increasingly, people are making advance arrangements for their own funeral and burial. This makes it easier on the family both financially and emotionally. All decisions have been made and there is no guessing what the decedent would have wanted.

If the decedent made provision for his burial space, then you need to locate the burial certificate. If the decedent purchased a preneed funeral plan, then you need to locate the contract. You should read the contract to determine what provisions were made. Some contracts are paid on an installment basis. If the decedent signed such a contract, then you need to find out what monies were paid and whether there is a remaining balance due.

If you cannot locate the contract, but you know the name of the funeral home, then call and ask them to send you a copy of the contract. If you believe the decedent purchased a funeral plan but you do not know the name of the funeral home, then call the local funeral homes. Many local funeral homes are owned by national firms with computer capacity to identify people who have purchased a contract in any of their many locations.

Once you have possession of the contract, bring it with you to the funeral home and go over the terms of the contract with the funeral director. Inquire whether there will be any charge that is not included in the contract.

MAKING FUNERAL ARRANGEMENTS

If the decedent died unexpectedly or without having made any prior funeral arrangements, then your first job is to choose a funeral director and make arrangements for the funeral or cremation. Most people choose the nearest or most conveniently located funeral home without comparison shopping, however prices for these services can vary significantly from funeral home to funeral home. Savings can be had if you take the time to make a few phone calls.

Receiving price quotes by telephone is your right under Federal law. Federal Trade Commission ("FTC") Rule 453.2 (b) (1) requires a funeral director to give an accurate telephone quote of the prices of his goods and services. Funeral homes are listed in the telephone directory under FUNERAL DIRECTORS. If you live in a small town, there may be only one or two listings. If such is the case, then check out some funeral homes in the next largest city.

Funeral Directors usually provide the following services:
➤ obtain burial and transit permits
➤ arrange for the transportation of the body
   to the funeral home and then to the burial site
➤ arrange for the embalming or cremation of the body
➤ arrange funeral and memorial services
➤ file the death certificate and order copies for the family
➤ have memorial and acknowledgment cards printed
➤ arrange to print the obituary

To compare prices you will need to determine:

✧ what is included in the price of a basic funeral plan

✧ whether you can expect any additional cost.

Embalming may be necessary if you are going to have a viewing. Embalming is not necessary if you order a direct cremation or an immediate burial. Federal Trade Commission Rule 453.5 prohibits the funeral home from charging an embalming fee unless you order the service.

If the decedent did not own a burial space, then that cost must be included when making funeral arrangements.

PURCHASING THE CASKET

When comparison-shopping, you will find that the single most expensive item in the funeral arrangement is the casket. Most funeral directors will quote you a price for the basic funeral plan. That plan does not include the cost of the casket. Directors usually quote a range of prices for the casket, saying that you will need to come in and choose the casket at the time you contract for the funeral.

When selecting a casket you should be aware that there is a considerable markup in the price quoted by the funeral director. You do not need to deal "sole source" when purchasing a the casket. You can purchase a casket elsewhere and have it delivered to the funeral home for use instead of the one offered by the funeral director.

In 1994, The Federal Trade Commission ruled that funeral homes had to accept caskets purchased elsewhere. (FTC Rule 453.4). The ruling includes a ban on funeral homes charging a handling fee for accepting a casket purchased elsewhere.

If you wish to shop for a casket, then the best time to do so is before you go to the funeral home to arrange for the funeral. You can find a retail casket sales outlet in the telephone book under CASKETS. You may need to look in the telephone directory for the nearest large city to find a listing. For users of the Internet, you can use your search engine to find the retail sales casket company nearest you. By making a call to a retail casket sales dealer, you will become knowledgeable in the price range of caskets. You can then decide what is a reasonable price for the product you seek.

Once you have determined what you should pay for the casket, it is only fair to give the funeral director the opportunity to meet that price. If you cannot reach a meeting of the minds, then you can always order the casket from the retail sales dealer and have it delivered to the funeral home.

ON-LINE FUNERAL SERVICES

The Internet is changing the way the world does business, and the funeral industry is no exception. A growing number of mortuaries are offering live Webcasts of funerals and wakes for those who are unable to pay their respects in person.

There are Web sites such as ObitDetails.com where you can post an obituary. There are online memorials chat rooms as well as online eulogies and testimonials. There is even a Web site that offers a posthumous e-mail service which allows people to leave final messages for friends and relatives.

THE CREMATION

Increasingly people are opting for cremation. The reasons for choosing cremation are varied, but for the majority, it is a matter of finances. The cost of cremation is approximately one-sixth that of an ordinary funeral and burial. A major saving is the cost of the casket. No casket is necessary for the cremation. Federal law prohibits a Funeral Director from saying that a casket is required for a direct cremation (FTC Rule 453.3 (b)ii). Of course if you want to have a viewing of the body and/or a funeral service with the body present, then you may need to purchase a disposable casket made of wood or cardboard, or you can rent a casket from the Funeral Director.

If you are having a memorial service in a place of worship with no viewing of the body before the cremation, then consider contracting with a facility that does cremations only. Look in the telephone book under CREMATION SERVICES. You will also see cremation "societies" in the telephone book. Some are for-profit and others not-for-profit. You can also find advertisements for cremation services on the Internet. These cremation facilities provide much the same services as a funeral home but with one important exception — the cremation service does not provide any type of funeral service or public viewing of the body.

 THE OVERWEIGHT DECEDENT

If the decedent weighs more than 300 pounds, then you need to check to see if the Cremation service has facilities large enough to handle the body. If you cannot locate a crematory that can accommodate the body, then you need to make burial arrangements.

DISPOSING OF THE ASHES

The decedent's cremains can be place in a cemetery plot. Many cemeteries have a separate building called *columbarium*, which is especially designed to store urns. Some cemeteries allow the cremains of a family member to be placed in a plot or mausoleum currently occupied by a member of the decedent's family. If it is your desire to have the cremains placed in an occupied family plot or mausoleum, then you need to call the cemetery and ask them to explain their policy as it relates to the burial of urns in occupied sites.

If the cremains are to be placed in a cemetery, then you need to obtain a suitable urn for the burial. You can purchase the urn from the Funeral Director or Crematory Service Director. Urns cost much less than caskets, but they can cost several hundred dollars. You may wish to do some comparison shopping by calling a retail sales casket dealer.

The decedent may have expressed a desire that his ashes be spread out to sea. The Funeral Director or Cremation Service Director can assist you with such arrangements, or you can do so yourself. You can use a boat or airplane to scatter the cremains at sea. North Carolina statute allows cremains to be spread over any uninhabited public land. If you wish to scatter them on private property, you first obtain permission from the owner of the property (NCGS 90-210.46 (c)(f)).

If you order a cremation and neglect to pick up the cremains or arrange for their disposition, then after 30 days from the date of the cremation, the crematory or funeral director may dispose of the cremains and then charge you for the cost of their disposition (NCGS 90-210.46 (b)).

SPOUSE	➤	THE MILITARY BURIAL

Subject to availability of burial spaces, an honorably discharged veteran and/or his unmarried minor or handicapped child and/or his un-remarried spouse may be buried in a national military cemetery. Some cemeteries have room only for cremated remains or for the casketed remains of a family member of someone who is currently buried in that cemetery, so you will need to call to check for space availability.

There are four national military cemeteries in North Carolina:

New Bern National Cemetery   (919) 637-2912
Raleigh National Cemetery   (704) 636-2661
Salisbury National Cemetery   (704) 636-2661
Wilmington National Cemetery   (919) 637-2912

and 3 state military cemeteries:

Western Carolina State Vet. Cem.   (828) 669-0684
Old Highway 70; Black Mountain, NC 28711

Coastal Carolina State Veterans Cemetery (910) 347-4550
P.O. Box 1486, Jacksonville, NC 28541

Sandshills State Veterans Cemetery   (910) 436-5630
P.O. Box 39, Spring Lake, NC 28390

The Department of the Army is in charge of the Arlington National Cemetery. If you wish to have an eligible deceased veteran buried in the Arlington National Cemetery, then call them at (703) 695-3250.

Arlington National Cemetery
Interment Service Branch
Arlington, VA 22211

THE COST OF A MILITARY BURIAL

Burial space in a National Cemetery is free of charge. Cemetery employees will open and close the grave and mark it with headstone or grave marker without cost to the family. The local Veteran's Administration ("VA") will provide the family with a memorial flag. The family needs to make funeral arrangements with a funeral firm and have them transport the remains to the cemetery.

If the decedent was receiving a VA pension then the VA will pay a burial and funeral expense allowance regardless of where the veteran is buried. The VA will not reimburse any burial or funeral cost for the spouse of a veteran.

For information about reimbursement of funeral and burial expenses you can call the VA at (800) 827-1000.

The Department of Veteran's Affairs has a Web site with information on the following topics:

> ➤ National and Military Cemeteries
> ➤ Burial, Headstones and Markers
> ➤ State Cemetery Grants Program
> ➤ Obtaining Military Records
> ➤ Locating Veterans

 VA CEMETERY WEB SITE
http://www.cem.va.gov

BENEFITS FOR SPOUSE OF DECEDENT VETERAN

If the decedent was honorably discharged, then regardless of where he is buried, his spouse might be eligible for a contribution from the Veteran's Administration for his funeral and burial expenses. If the decedent had minor or disabled children, his spouse may also be eligible for a monthly benefit of Dependency and Indemnity Compensation ("DIC").

If the Veteran's surviving spouse receives nursing home care under Medicaid, then the spouse might be eligible for a monthly payment from the VA. Whether the surviving spouse is eligible for any of these benefits depends on many factors including whether the decedent was serving on active duty, whether his death was service related, and the surviving spouse's assets and income.

For information about whether the surviving spouse is eligible for any benefit related to the decedent's military service, call the VETERANS ADMINISTRATION at (800) 827-1000.

You can receive a printed statement of public policy: VA Pamphlet 051-000-00217-2 FEDERAL BENEFITS FOR VETERANS AND DEPENDENTS by sending a check in the amount of $5 to
THE SUPERINTENDENT OF DOCUMENTS
P.O. Box 371954
Pittsburgh, PA 15250-7954
Information is also available on the VA web site:

 VA WEB SITE
http://www.va.gov

If the decedent is to be buried in another state, then the body will need to be transported to that state. Most funeral firms belong to a national network of funeral firms, and the out-of-state funeral director has the means to make local arrangements to ship the body. Contact the out-of-state funeral director and have him/her make arrangement with the airline for the transportation of the body.

If services are to be held in North Carolina and in another state, then contact the local funeral firm and they will make arrangements with the out-of-state funeral firm to transport the body.

If the body has been cremated, then you can transport the ashes yourself, either by carrying the ashes as part of your luggage or by arranging with the airline to transport the ashes as cargo. You should have a certified copy of the death certificate available in the event that you need to identify the cremains of the decedent. Call the airline before departure and ask whether they have any special regulation or procedure regarding the transportation of human ashes.

Special Situation → THE VIOLENT DEATH

If the decedent died a violent death or under circumstances in which foul play is suspected, the Medical Examiner will take possession of the body. The body will not be released to the funeral director until the examination of the body is complete. In the interim, the family can proceed with arrangements for the funeral. The funeral director will contact the Medical Examiner to determine when he can pick up the body and proceed with the funeral.

If the decedent died because of a criminal act and you are a family member, then you may wish to contact an attorney experienced in Criminal Law tolearn of your rights as a family member. If the perpetrator of the crime has significant funds, you may want to sue for a wrongful death.

 LAWYER   THE ACCIDENTAL DEATH

If the decedent died because of an accident, then it is important to contact a Personal Injury attorney to determine whether the family has a case for wrongful death. If the accident was related to the decedent's job, the family may wish to consult with a Worker's Compensation attorney as well.

| Special Situation | CRIME VICTIM COMPENSATION |

If the decedent died because of a criminal act and you are a family member, then you may be eligible to receive compensation under the NORTH CAROLINA CRIME VICTIMS COMPENSATION ACT. Subject to the amount of money appropriated by the North Carolina Assembly, the state can provide compensation for reasonable funeral expenses (up to $3,500), and for medical care for the victim (up to $30,000). To be eligible the following must be true:

➤ The decedent was an innocent victim (i.e., did not do anything wrong).

➤ The crime was reported to authorities within 72 hours of its commission or discovery of the body.

➤ Application for compensation was filed within two years from the date of the crime.

➤ There are no other resources, such as health or life insurance, available to cover medical or burial costs. (NCGS 15 B-11, 15 B-25).

It may take several weeks for the North Carolina Victim Compensation Commission to process the claim, but if you need emergency funds (i.e., for the burial), then they can release monies and credit that amount toward the final award.

To receive an application for compensation and an information pamphlet call (800) 826-6200. Out of state call (919) 733-7974 or you can write to:

Division of Victim and Justice Services
4703 Mail Service Center
Raleigh, NC 27699-4703

| Special
| Situation   >   THE UNCLAIMED BODY

Each agency in charge of receiving a body (police, hospital, etc.) will make every reasonable effort to identify the body and notify the family of the death. If the body is unclaimed for 10 days, then the agency will offer the body to the Commission of Anatomy. The state of North Carolina created the Commission to promote the study of anatomy. If the body is accepted, the Commission will donate the body to any one of the four schools of medicine located within the state (see page 6). If they do not accept the body, then the county's Director of Social Services will arrange for the burial or cremation (NCGS 130A-33.30, 130A-415).

THE INDIGENT DECEDENT

If an indigent person dies and the police can determine his identity, they will try to locate the family. If the decedent is an indigent migrant agricultural worker, and his family is willing to take responsibility for the disposition of the body, but they do not have sufficient funds to return his body to his legal residence, then the county Department of Social Services, can pay up to $200 toward the cost of transportation (NCGS 130A-418).

If the indigent decedent is an honorably discharged veteran, then the Veteran's Administration will arrange for a burial. If the indigent person is not an honorably discharged veteran and/or his family is unable or unwilling to arrange for the burial, then the body is treated as any other unclaimed body and is offered to the Commission to be donated for study.

 **LAWYER** | # THE MISSING BODY

Few things are more difficult to deal with than a missing person. The emotional turmoil created by the "not knowing" is often more difficult than the finality of death. The legal problems created by the disappearance are also more difficult than if the person simply died:

APPOINTING THE RECEIVER

If a person is missing and cannot be found after a diligent search, then that person is referred to as an *absentee*. If the absentee has business matters that need attending (bills that need to be paid, checks that need to be cashed, etc.), then anytime after 30 days from the disappearance, anyone can *petition* (ask) the Superior Court to appoint a Receiver to handle the absentee's affairs. You will need to employ an attorney who is experienced in probate matters to get the Receiver appointed.

If the circumstances of the disappearance are sufficient to justify the belief that the missing person is dead or after 5 years have passed, whichever is earlier, the judge will take further evidence to determine whether the Receivership should be terminated. If the judge finds that the absentee is probably dead, he will then determine if there is a valid Will. If there is a valid Will, he will order the Receiver to make a final accounting and distribute the funds according to the Will. If there is no Will, he will order the property distributed according to the Laws of Descent and Distribution. See Chapter 5 for an explanation of the law (NCGS 28C-2, 6, 11, 12).

THE PROBLEM
FUNERAL OR BURIAL

The funeral and burial industry is well regulated by the state and federal government. Under North Carolina statute, the following acts are subject to disciplinary action:

⊠ Delivering goods of a lesser quality than that presented to the purchaser as a sample.

⊠ Using a false or misleading advertisement.

⊠ Gross immorality, including being under the influence of alcohol or drugs while practicing funeral service.

⊠ Paying kick-backs to generate business.

⊠ Using profane, indecent or obscene language in the presence of a body or within hearing of the family.

⊠ Indecent exposure or exhibition of a body.

(NCGS 90-210.25(a)(5)(e1))

Funeral directors are licensed professionals so it is unusual to have a problem with the funeral or burial or cremation. If, however, you had a bad experience with any aspect of the funeral then you can file a complaint with the state licensing agency:

> North Carolina Board of Mortuary Science
> P.O. Box 27368
> Raleigh, NC   27611-7368
> Telephone: (919) 733-9380

 LAWYER

In addition to filing a complaint with the Board, you may wish to consult with an attorney who is experienced in litigation matters to learn of any other legal remedy that you may have.

THE DEATH CERTIFICATE

The Funeral Director or Cremation Service Director will order as many certified copies of the death certificate as you request. Most establishments require an original certified copy and not a photocopy so you need to order sufficient copies. The following is a list of institutions that may request a certified copy:

* Each insurance company that insured the decedent or his property (health insurance company, life insurance company, car insurance company, home insurance company)

* Each financial institution in which the decedent had money invested (brokerage houses, banks)

* The decedent's pension fund

* Each credit card company used by the decedent

* The IRS

* The Social Security Administration

* The Register of deeds in each county (other than the county of his residence) where the decedent owned real property.

* If probate is necessary, then the Clerk of the Superior Court where the probate is conducted.

Some airlines and car rental companies offer a discount for short notice, emergency trips. If you have family flying in for the funeral, you may wish to order a few extra copies of the death certificate so that they can obtain an airline or car rental discount.

ORDERING COPIES OF THE DEATH CERTIFICATE

If you wish to order certified copies of the death certificate at a later date, you can call the funeral director and ask him to do so or you can write and request a copy from the local Registrar in the county of the decedent's residence or from the State Registrar at the following address:

North Carolina Vital Records
1903 Mail Service Center
Raleigh, NC 27699-1903
Telephone: (919) 733-3000   Fax: (919) 733-1511

The local and State Registrar will issue a certified copy of the death certificate only to members of the decedent's family (spouse, sibling, child, stepchild parent, grandparent, stepparent), the Personal Representative or his attorney. The current charge is $10 per certified copy. You may save time by first calling and asking what information is required.

RECORDING THE DEATH CERTIFICATE
The original death certificate is kept with the State Registrar. The local Registrar keeps a copy of the certificate and forwards a copy to the County Register of Deeds. If the decedent lived within county limits, the County Register of Deeds will keep a record of the death certificate on file. If the decedent owned real property in the county of his residence, then anyone who is doing a title search will learn of the death (NCGS 130A-93, 130A-97(5), 130A-99).

 **OUT OF STATE PROPERTY**

If the decedent owned property in another state, then a death certificate may need to be recorded in the county where that property is located. Not all states require that the death certificate be recorded. You may want to call the Clerk to determine whether a death certificate needs to be recorded. In some states the county Recorder or the Clerk of the Circuit Court is in charge of recording deeds (and death certificates).

If you find that a death certificate needs to be recorded, it is prudent to contact an attorney in the state where the property is located for advice about what other documents may need to be recorded in order to complete the transfer the decedent's real property in that state.

About Probate

Once a person dies, all of the property he owns as of the date of his death is referred to as the *decedent's estate.* If the decedent owned property that was in his name only (not jointly or in trust for someone), then some sort of court procedure is necessary to determine who is entitled to possession of the property. The name of the court procedure is *Probate.*

The root of the word probate is "to prove." It refers to the first job of the probate court, that is, to examine proof of whether the decedent left a valid Will, i.e. he died *testate* or whether he died *intestate* (without a valid Will). The second job of the probate court is to appoint someone to wrap up the affairs of the decedent — to pay any outstanding bills and then to distribute what property is left to the beneficiaries.

If the decedent named someone in his Will to be the *Executor* of his estate, then the court will appoint that person for the job and issue *Letters Testamentary* giving him authority to administer the estate. If the decedent died intestate, then the court will appoint someone to be the *Administrator* of the his estate and issue *Letters of Administration.* The term *Personal Representative* is used to represent anyone who has the job of settling the decedent's estate. For simplicity we will use that term, and we will refer to the document authorizing him to act, as *Letters* (NCGS 28A-4-1).

There are different ways to conduct a probate procedure depending on the value of the property that being probated, and whether the decedent owned real property at the time of his death. We will refer to the property being probated as the decedent's *Probate Estate* and the method of conducting a probate procedure the *Estate Administration*. Chapter 6 explains the different kinds of estate administration that are available in Florida.

But we are getting ahead of ourselves. First we need to determine whether a probate procedure is necessary. To answer that question we need to know exactly what the decedent owned, so the next two chapters explain how to identify, and then locate, all of the decedent's assets.

Giving Notice Of The Death 2

Those closest to the decedent usually notify family members and close friends by telephone. The funeral director will arrange to have an obituary published in as many different newspapers as the family requests, but there is still the job of notifying the government and people who were doing business with the decedent. That task belongs to the person named as the Executor in the decedent's Will. If the decedent died without a Will, then the spouse has the right to be appointed as Personal Representative. If there is no spouse, or if the spouse is unable or unwilling to serve, then anyone who has the right to inherit the decedent's property can be appointed. When two or more persons are qualified, the Clerk of the Superior Court will determine who is most likely to administer the estate advantageously (NCGS 28A-4-1).

If no probate procedure is necessary, the job of notifying people of the death and settling the decedent's affairs falls to his spouse; and in the absence of a spouse, to the decedent's next of kin. By *next of kin,* we mean those people who inherit the decedent's property according to the NORTH CAROLINA LAWS OF DESCENT AND DISTRIBUTION. Those laws are explained in Chapter 5.

The person who has the job of settling the decedent's estate should begin to give notice as soon as is practicable after the death. Two government agencies that need to be notified are the Social Security Administration and the IRS. This chapter gives their telephone number as well as those of all the other agencies that need to be notified.

NOTIFYING SOCIAL SECURITY

Many Funeral Directors will, as part of their service package, notify the Social Security Administration of the death. You may wish to check to see that this has been done. You can do so by calling (800) 772-1213. If you are hearing impaired call (800) 325-0778 TTY. You will need to give the Social Security Administration the full legal name of the decedent as well as his social security number and date of birth.

Special Situation > DECEDENT RECEIVING SOCIAL SECURITY CHECKS

If the decedent was receiving checks from Social Security, then you need to determine whether his last check needs to be returned to the Social Security Administration.

Each Social Security check is a payment for the prior month, provided that person lives for the entire prior month. If someone dies on the last day of the month, then you should not cash the check for that month. For example, if someone dies on July 31st, then you need to return the check that the agency mails out in August. If however, the decedent died on August 1st then the check sent in August need not be returned because that check is payment for the month of July.

If the Social Security check is electronically deposited into a bank account then notify the bank that the account holder died and notify the Social Security Administration as well. If the check needs to be returned, then the Social Security Administration will withdraw it electronically from the bank account. You will need to keep the account open until the funds are withdrawn.

 ## SPOUSE/CHILD'S SOCIAL SECURITY BENEFITS

If the decedent had sufficient work credits, the Social Security Administration will give the decedent's widow(er) or if unmarried, then the decedent's minor children, a one-time death benefit in the amount of $255.

SURVIVORS BENEFITS:

The spouse (or ex-spouse) of the decedent may be eligible for Survivors Benefits. Benefits vary depending on the amount of work credits earned by the decedent; whether the decedent had minor or disabled children; the spouse's age; how long they were married; etc.

The minor child of the decedent may be eligible for dependent child's benefits regardless of whether the decedent father ever married the child's mother. Paternity can be established by any one of several methods including the father acknowledging his child in writing or verbally to members of his family.

SOCIAL SECURITY BENEFITS

A spouse or ex-spouse can collect social security benefits based on the decedent's work record. This value may be greater than the spouse now receives. It is important to make an appointment with your local Social Security office and determine whether you as the spouse (or ex-spouse) or parent of decedent's minor child are eligible for any Social Security or Survivor benefit. The Social Security Administration has a web site from which you can down load publications that explain survivors benefits:

 SOCIAL SECURITY WEB SITE
http://www.ssa.gov

| Special Situation | DECEDENT WITH GOVERNMENT PENSION |

If the decedent was a federal retiree and received a government pension then any check received after the date of death needs to be returned to the U.S. Treasury. If the check is direct deposited to a bank account, then call the financial institution and ask them to return the check. If the check is sent by mail then you need to return it to: Director, Regional Finance Center
U. S. Treasury Department
P.O. Box 7367
Chicago, IL 60680
Include a letter explaining the reason for the return of the check and stating the decedent's date of death.

$$$ APPLY FOR BENEFITS $$$

Even though you notify the government of the death, they will not automatically give you benefits to which you may be entitled. You need to apply for those benefits by notifying the Office of Personnel Management ("OPM") of the death and requesting that they send you an application for survivor benefits. You can call them at (888) 767-6738 or you can write to:
THE OFFICE OF PERSONNEL MANAGEMENT
SERVICE AND RECORDS CENTER
BOYERS, PA 16017
You will find brochures and information about Survivor's Benefits at the OPM Web site:

OFFICE OF PERSONNEL MANAGEMENT WEB SITE
http://www.opm.gov
You can get assistance via E-mail at
retire@opm.gov

DECEDENT WITH COMPANY PENSION OR ANNUITY

In most cases, pension and annuity checks are payment for the prior month. If the decedent received his pension or annuity check before his death, then no monies need be returned. Pension checks and/or annuity checks received after the date of death may need to be returned to the company. You need to notify the company of the death to determine the status of the last check sent to the decedent.

Before notifying the company, locate the policy or pension statement that is the basis of the income. That document should tell whether there is a beneficiary of the pension or annuity funds now that the pensioner or annuitant is dead. If you cannot locate the document, use the return address on the check envelope and ask the company to send you a copy of the plan. Also request that they forward to you any claim form that may be required in order for the survivor or beneficiary to receive benefits under that pension plan or policy.

If the pension/annuity check is direct deposited to the decedent's account, then ask the bank to assist you in locating the company and notifying the company of the death.

DECEDENT WITH AN IRA
or QUALIFIED RETIREMENT PLAN

Anyone who is a beneficiary of an Individual Retirement Account ("IRA") or Qualified Retirement Plan ("QRP") needs to keep in mind is that no income taxes have been paid on monies placed in the account. Once monies are withdrawn, significant taxes may be due. You need to learn what options are available to you as a beneficiary of the plan and the tax consequences of each option. You will need to ask an accountant how much will be due in taxes for each option. Once you know all the facts, you will be able to make the best choice for your circumstance.

 **SPOUSE** If the spouse is the beneficiary of the decedent's IRA account, then there are special options available. The spouse has the right to withdraw the money from the account or roll it over into the spouse's own retirement account. Although the employer can explain options that are available, the spouse still needs to understand the tax consequence of choosing any given option. It is important to consult with an accountant to determine the best way to go.

If the decedent had a QRP, the plan may permit the spouse to roll the balance of the account into a new IRA. The spouse needs to contact the decedent's employer for an explanation of the plan and all the options that are available at this time.

NOTIFYING IRS

THE FINAL INCOME TAX RETURN

The Personal Representative, or next of kin, needs to file the decedent's final federal and state income tax return. Filing the final return is done as part of filing the income tax return for the year of his death. If you have a joint bank account with the decedent, do not close that account until you determine whether the decedent is entitled to an income tax refund. See Chapter 6 for an explanation of how to obtain a refund from the IRS.

THE GOOD NEWS

Monies inherited from the decedent are generally not counted as income to you, so you do not pay federal income tax on those monies. If the monies you inherit later earn interest or income for you, then of course you will report that income as you do any other type of income.

Real and personal property inherited by a beneficiary is inherited at a "stepped up" basis. This means that if the decedent purchased some item that is now worth more than when he purchased it, then the beneficiary inherits the property at its fair market value as of the decedent's date of death. For example, suppose the decedent bought stock for $20,000 and it is now worth $50,000, then the beneficiary inherits the stock at the $50,000 value. If the beneficiary sells the stock for $50,000, he pays no tax. If the beneficiary holds onto the stock and later sells it for $60,000, the beneficiary will pay federal capital gains tax only on the $10,000 increase in value since the decedent's death.

| SPOUSE | SELLING THE HOME |

In the tough "ole days" the IRS used to allow a once-in-a-lifetime, over age 55, up to $125,000 capital gains tax exclusion on the sale of the homestead (the principal residence). If a married couple sold their home and took the exclusion it was "used up" and no longer available to the other partner. In these, the good times, the IRS allows you to sell your homestead and up to $250,000 ($500,000 for a married couple) of the home-sale profit is tax free (IRC Section 121 B 3). There is no limit on the number of times you can use the exemption, provided you own and live in the homestead at least 2 years prior to the sale.

If the decedent and his spouse used their "once in a lifetime" homestead tax exemption, with this new law, the surviving spouse can sell the homestead and once again take advantage of a tax break.

FEDERAL AND STATE ESTATE TAXES

An *estate tax* is a tax imposed by the federal and state government for the transfer of property at death. The *taxable estate* of the decedent is the total value of all of his property, as of his date of death. This includes real property (homestead, vacant lots, etc.) and personal property (cars, life insurance policies, business interests, securities, IRA accounts, etc.). It includes property held in the decedent's name alone, as well as property that he held jointly or in trust for another.

The Federal government gives each person an Estate and Gift Tax Exclusion amount. No gift tax need be paid unless the decedent's taxable estate, plus gifts that he gave during his lifetime that exceeded $10,000 per person, per year, exceed the Exclusion amount. The Exclusion amount is scheduled to increase each year until the year 2006:

YEAR	EXCLUSION AMOUNT
2000 — 2001	$675,000
2002 — 2003	$700,000
2004	$850,000
2005	$950,000
2006	$1,000,000

No Federal Estate tax return need be filed unless the decedent's taxable estate and lifetime gifts exceed the scheduled amount as of his date of death. There is an unlimited marital tax deduction, so if the decedent was married, no estate tax need be paid, however if the decedent's estate exceeds the stated value, an estate tax return must be filed.

The North Carolina estate tax due is a percentage of the Federal tax credit (NCGS 105-32.2). The computation of the estate tax is complex. It is advisable to seek the counsel of an accountant or tax attorney to prepare both the state and federal return.

WHEN TO EVALUATE THE PROPERTY

When filing an estate tax return, the IRS gives you a choice of taking the value of the decedent's estate as of the date of death or 6 months later. The government's intent is to allow a reduction in estate taxes in the event that something happens during the 6 month period causing the property to lose its value. For example, suppose stock worth $500,000 is included as part of the decedent's estate. If the stock decreases to $400,000 within the 6 months following the death, then you can declare the $400,000 value. If the stock increases to $600,000, then you can still use the $500,000 date of death value.

The IRS does not allow the election unless the election will decrease the value of the gross estate and the total net estate taxes due. If there are little taxes due, then before deciding on a 6 month valuation date, you need to consider the cost of employing an accountant (or a tax attorney) to file the necessary tax forms. The cost in time and expense to make the election could be more than the tax payment itself. And there is the more important consideration of the risk of holding onto the stock should the Bull market morph into a Bear. Paying less in taxes is small consolation for a sizeable loss in the value of the securities.

GIFT TAX FOR EVERYONE (except the spouse)

The state of North Carolina imposes a gift tax on all gifts made within the state in excess of $10,000 per person per year. If the decedent made a gift in excess of $10,000 in any given year, then he was required to report that gift on his annual return. If gifts were given to the decedent's **descendants** (children, grandchildren, etc.) or **ascendants** (parents, grandparents, etc.), then no tax is due unless the total value of gifts given to that person (before and after death) exceeds $100,000. As with the Federal Estate and Gift tax, there is an unlimited marital deduction, meaning that no taxes are due on gifts to the decedent's spouse. Gifts to the state or to charitable, religious, or educational institutions located within the state are also exempt.

The amount of gift tax due depends on the relationship of the beneficiary to the decedent and the value of the gift. For the decedent's ascendants and descendants the rate is 1% for the first $10,000 over the $100,000 exemption. It graduates to 4% on $200,000, with a maximum tax rate of 12% for gifts over 3 million dollars. For brothers, sisters and their descendants; and the decedent's aunts and uncles, the rate is 4% for the first $5,000, graduating to 10% on $250,00; to a maximum 16% for gifts over 3 million. For gifts to everyone else, the rate starts at 8% on the first $10,000; and graduates to 17% for gifts over 2.5 million.

If the beneficiary of the property is not a resident of the state, then the tax applies only to property located within the state. For example, if the decedent's son does not live in North Carolina, and he inherits the decedent's land in Maine, then the gift is not taxable in North Carolina (it might be taxable in Maine). But if the decedent leaves his son land in North Carolina, then the gift is taxable (NCGS 105-188, 105-197).

DECEDENT WITH A TRUST

If the decedent was the Grantor (or Settlor) of a trust, then he was probably managing the trust as Trustee during his lifetime. The trust document should name a *Successor Trustee* to manage the trust now that the Grantor is deceased. The trust document may instruct the Successor Trustee to make certain distributions, or gifts once the Grantor dies or the trust document may direct the Successor Trustee to hold money in trust for some beneficiary.

☎ LAWYER

IF YOU ARE SUCCESSOR TRUSTEE

If you are the Successor Trustee then in addition to following the terms of the trust, you are required to obey all of the laws of the state of North Carolina relating to the administration of the trust. For example, the law prohibits any self dealing or conflicts of interest. For example you cannot buy or sell property for yourself. The law also bars indirect purchases, such as a purchase of trust property by the Trustee's spouse (NCGS 36A-66). You should consult with an attorney experienced in Estate Planning to explain to you how to properly administer the trust to make sure that you do so without any liability to yourself.

IF YOU ARE A BENEFICIARY

If you are a beneficiary of the trust, then you need to obtain a copy of the trust and see how the trust is to be administered now that the Grantor or Settlor is deceased. Most trust documents are written in "legalese," so you may want to employ your own attorney to review the trust, and explain what rights you have under that trust.

NOTIFYING THE BUSINESS COMMUNITY

People and companies who were doing business with the decedent need to be notified of his death. This includes utility companies, credit card companies, banks, brokerage firms and any company that insured the decedent.

NOTIFY CREDIT CARD COMPANIES

You need to notify the decedent's credit card companies of the death. If you can find the contract with the credit card company check to see whether the decedent had credit card insurance. If the decedent had credit card insurance, then the balance of the account is now paid in full. If you cannot find the contract contact the company and get a copy of the contract along with a statement of the balance due as of the date of death.

DESTROY DECEDENT'S CREDIT CARDS
You need to destroy all of the decedent's credit cards. If you hold a credit card jointly with the decedent, then it is important to waste no time in closing that account and opening another in your name only.

That's something Barbara knows from hard experience. She and Hank lived together but never married. She took care of Hank at home when he became ill with hepatitis. Hank came from a well to do family. They supported the couple during Hank's long illness. Hank put Barbara on all of his credit card accounts so that she could purchase things when he became too ill to go shopping with her.

After the funeral, Barbara had a gathering of friends and family at their apartment. Barbara was so preoccupied with her loss that she never noticed that Hank's credit cards were missing until the bills started coming in.

Barbara did not know who ran up the bills on Hank's credit cards during the month following his death. It was obvious that Hank's signature had been forged — but who forged it? One credit card company suspected that it might have been Barbara herself.

Because the cards were held jointly, it was Barbara's responsibility to straighten out the mess. Most of her credit card contracts required that she pay a fee of $50 for an unauthorized use of the card. She was able to clear her credit record but it took several weeks and hundreds of dollars to do so.

NOTIFY INSURANCE COMPANIES

Examine the decedent's financial records to determine the name and telephone number of all of the companies that insured the decedent or his property. This includes real property insurance, motor vehicle insurance, health insurance and life insurance.

MOTOR VEHICLE INSURANCE
If the decedent owned any type of motor vehicle (car, truck, boat, airplane) locate the insurance policy on that vehicle and notify the insurance company of the death. Determine how long insurance coverage continues after the death. Ask the insurance agent to explain what things are covered under the policy. Is the motor vehicle covered for all types of casualty (theft, accident, vandalism, etc.) or is coverage limited in some way? Determine when the next insurance payment is due. Hopefully, the car will be sold or transferred to a beneficiary before that date, but if not, then you need to arrange to continue with insurance coverage.

Special Situation   ACCIDENTAL DEATH

If the decedent died as a result of an accident, then check for all possible sources of accident insurance coverage including his homeowner's policy. Some credit card companies provide accident insurance as part of their contract with their card holders.

If the decedent died in an automobile accident, check to see whether he was covered by any type of travel insurance, such as rental car insurance. If he belonged to an automobile club, such as AAA, then check whether he had accident insurance as part of his club membership.

LIFE INSURANCE COMPANIES

If the decedent had life insurance, then you need to locate the policy and notify the company of his death. Call each life insurance company and ask what they require in order to forward the insurance proceeds to the beneficiary. Most companies will ask you to send them the original policy and a certified copy of the death certificate.

Send the original policy by certified mail or any of the overnight services that require a signed receipt for the package. Make a copy of the original policy for your records before mailing the original policy to the company.

IF YOU CANNOT LOCATE THE POLICY

If you know that the decedent was insured but you cannot locate the insurance policy, the AMERICAN COUNCIL OF LIFE INSURANCE ("ACLI") may be able to help you. Write to the ACLI giving them the name, address, date of birth, and social security number of the decedent. Their address is:

POLICY SEARCH ACLI
1000 Pennsylvania Avenue, NW
Washington, DC 20004

The ACLI will assist you by asking the 100 largest insurance companies in the nation to search their records for the missing policy. If it is found, you will receive a copy of the policy free of charge.

IF YOU CANNOT LOCATE THE COMPANY

If you cannot locate the insurance company it may be doing business under another name or it may no longer be doing business in the state of North Carolina. Each state has a branch of government that regulates insurance companies doing business in that state. If you are having difficulty locating the insurance company call the Department of Insurance in the state where the policy was purchased and ask for assistance in locating the company. The number for the North Carolina Department of Insurance is (919)733-7343. Within the state of North Carolina call (800) 662-7777.

EAGLE PUBLISHING COMPANY OF BOCA has the telephone number for the Department of Insurance for each state at their Web site:

 EAGLE PUBLISHING COMPANY OF BOCA WEB SITE
http://www.eaglepublishing.com

WORK RELATED INSURANCE

If the decedent was employed then his employer may provide survivor benefits from a company or group life insurance plan and/or a retirement plan. If the decedent belonged to a union, then check with the union to determine whether members of the union receive any death benefits.

The decedent may have belonged to a professional, fraternal or social organization such as the local Chamber of Commerce, a Veteran's organization, the Kiwanis, AARP, the Rotary Club, etc. If he belonged to any such organization check to see whether the organization provided any type of insurance coverage.

 *Special Situation* BUSINESS OWNED BY DECEDENT

If the decedent owned his own company he may have purchased "key man" insurance. Key man insurance is a policy designed to protect the company should a valuable employee become disabled or die. Benefits are paid to the company to compensate the company for the loss of someone who is essential to the continuation of the business. Ultimately the policy benefits those who inherit the business.

If the decedent owned shares in the company or was a partner in the company, there may be a shareholder's agreement or partnership agreement that requires the company to use the insurance proceeds to purchase the decedent's shares or partnership interest. If there is a probate procedure, then the Personal Representative's attorney will need to review the agreement. If no probate is necessary then the next of kin need to find out what rights (if any) the family has in the business or to the proceeds of the key man insurance policy.

Special Situation → CORPORATE OFFICER OR REGISTERED AGENT

If the decedent was the sole officer and Registered Agent of the company, then the North Carolina Corporations Division needs to be notified of the identity of the new officers and Registered Agent. The law requires each corporation to continuously maintain a Registered Agent who resides in this state. A new Agent will need to be appointed as soon as is practicable (NCGS 55-5-01, 55-5-02).

Forms to change officers, directors and registered agents can be obtained by calling the North Carolina Secretary of State at their toll-free number:
(888) 246-7636
or by writing to: North Carolina Secretary of State
300 North Salisbury Street
Raleigh, NC 27603-5909

If you were not actively involved in running the business, then you might request a status report of the company. The report will show whether filing fees are current and will identify the officers and directors of the company. The North Carolina Secretary of State has a Web site from which you can download forms and obtain information about North Carolina corporations.

 NORTH CAROLINA CORPORATION WEB SITE
http://www.state.nc.us/secstate/

HOMEOWNER'S INSURANCE

If the decedent owned his own home, then check whether there is sufficient insurance coverage on the property. The decedent may have neglected to increase his insurance as the property appreciated in value. If you think the property may be vacant for some period of time, then it is important to have vandalism coverage included in the policy. Once the property is sold, or transferred to the proper beneficiary, you can have the policy discontinued or transferred to the new owner. The decedent's estate should receive a rebate for the unused portion of the premium.

MORTGAGE INSURANCE

If the decedent had a mortgage on any parcel of real estate that he owned, he might have arranged with his lender for an insurance policy that pays off the mortgage balance in the event of his death. Look at the closing statement to see if there was a charge for mortgage insurance. Also, check with the lender to determine if such a policy was purchased.

If the decedent was the sole owner of the property, then the beneficiary of that property needs to make arrangements to continue payment of the mortgage until title to the property is transferred to that beneficiary.

NOTIFY CONDO/HOMEOWNER ASSOCIATION

If the decedent owned a condominium or a residence regulated by a homeowner's association, then the association will need to be notified of the death. Once the property is transferred to the proper beneficiary, he/she will need to contact the association to learn of the rules and regulations regarding ownership and to arrange to have notices of dues and assessments forwarded to the new owner.

HEALTH INSURANCE

The Health Insurance carrier probably knows of the death, but it is a good idea to contact them to determine what coverage the decedent had under that insurance plan. If you cannot find the original policy, have the insurance company send you a copy of the policy so that you can determine whether medical treatment given to the decedent before his death was covered by that policy.

 **DECEDENT ON MEDICARE**

If the decedent was insured under Medicare then you do not need to notify anyone of the death, however, you do need to know what things were covered by Medicare so that you can determine what medical bills are (or are not) covered by Medicare. You can get the publication MEDICARE AND YOU by writing to:

U.S. GOVERNMENT PRINTING OFFICE
U.S. Dept. of Health and Human Services
Health Care Financing Administration
7500 Security Boulevard
Baltimore, MD 21244-1850

You can find HEALTH CARE AND YOU and other information about Medicare on the Internet:

 MEDICARE WEB SITE
http:/www.medicare.gov

THE SPOUSE'S HEALTH INSURANCE

SPOUSE ▶

If the spouse of the decedent is insured under Medicare, then the death does not affect the surviving spouse's coverage. If spouse was not covered by Medicare but has her own health insurance that also covered the decedent, then the spouse needs to notify the employer of the death because this may affect the cost of the plan to the employer and/or the spouse.

If the spouse was covered under the decedent's policy then he/she needs to arrange for new coverage. There are state and federal laws that ensure continued coverage under the decedent's policy for a period of time depending on whether the decedent's employer falls under federal or state regulation.

If the decedent was employed by a federally regulated company (usually a company with at least twenty employees) then under the Consolidated Omnibus Budget Reconciliation Act ("COBRA") the employer must make the company health plan available to the surviving spouse and any dependent child of the decedent for at least 36 months. The employer is required to give notice to the surviving spouse that the spouse and/or dependent child have the right to continue coverage under the decedent's health plan. The spouse and/or child have 60 days from the date of death or 60 days after the employer sends notice (whichever is later) to tell the employer whether the surviving spouse and child wish to continue with the health insurance plan.

SPOUSE'S HEALTH INSURANCE (continued)

The only problem with continued coverage may be the cost. Before the death, the employer may have been paying some percentage of the premium. The employer has no such duty after the death unless there was some employment agreement stating otherwise. Under COBRA, the employer may charge the spouse for the full cost of the plan plus a 2% administrative fee.

You can find additional information about COBRA in the publication PENSION AND HEALTH CARE COVERAGE. This and other publications can be found at the U.S. Department of Labor Web site:

 DEPARTMENT OF LABOR WEB SITE
http://www.dol.gov/dol/pwba

CONTINUED COVERAGE UNDER NC LAW

If the decedent's employer is not regulated under COBRA, then company's insurance coverage may be regulated under North Carolina law. The North Carolina law regulating health insurance is similar to COBRA, but with different time constraints. Coverage need only continue for 18 months. The insurance policy may provide that the spouse and/or dependent child have only 30 days from the date of death to let the employer know that they wish to continue coverage, so they need to promptly notify the employer if they wish to continue. Again, cost may be a problem. As with COBRA, the spouse can be charged the full cost of the policy plus an additional 2%. The spouse may find it less costly to seek health insurance elsewhere (NCGS 58-53-5; 58-53-10; 58-53-35; 58-53-40).

NOTIFYING THE ADVERTISER

Probably the last in the world to learn of the decedent's death is the direct mail advertiser. Advertisers are nothing if not tenacious. It is not uncommon for advertisements to be mailed to the decedent for more than ten years after the death. It is not because the advertiser is trying to sell something to the decedent, but rather the people who prepare (and sell) mailing lists do not know that the person is dead.

Those who sell mailing lists may not be motivated to update the list because of the cost of doing the necessary research; and perhaps because the price of the mailing list is often based on the number of people on the list. Even those who compose their own list may decide it is less costly to mail to everyone, than take the time (and money) to update the list.

If it gives you pleasure to think of advertisers spending substantial sums for nothing, then that is what you should do (nothing). But for those of you who wince each time you see another piece of mail addressed to the decedent, you can write to the Direct Marketing Association and ask that his name be deleted from all mailing lists:

Mail Preference Service
Direct Marketing Association
P.O. Box 9008
Farmingdale, NY 11735

You will need to give them the decedent's complete address, including zip code and every name variation that the decedent may have used; for example:

Mr. Theodore James Jones
Ted Jones   Ted J. Jones
T. J. Jones   T. James Jones, etc.

✍ CHANGE BENEFICIARIES ✍

If the decedent was someone you named as beneficiary of your insurance policy, Will or trust, brokerage account or pension plan, then you may need to name another beneficiary in his place:

INSURANCE POLICY ✍

If you named the decedent as the primary beneficiary of your life insurance policy, then check to see whether you named a contingent (alternate) beneficiary in the event that the decedent did not survive you. If not, then you need to contact the insurance company and name a new beneficiary. If you did name a contingent beneficiary, then that person is now your primary beneficiary and you need to consider whether you wish to name a new contingent beneficiary at this time.

HEALTH INSURANCE POLICY ✍

If the decedent was covered under your health insurance policy, then your employer and the health insurer need to be notified of the death because this may affect the cost of the plan to you and/or your employer.

WILL OR TRUST ✍

Most Wills provide for a contingent beneficiary in the event that the person named as beneficiary dies first. If you named the decedent as your beneficiary, then check to see whether you named an alternate beneficiary. If not, you need to have your attorney revise your Will and name a new beneficiary.

Similarly, if you are the Grantor or Settlor of a trust and the decedent was one of the beneficiaries of your trust, then check the trust document to see if you named an alternate beneficiary. If not, contact your attorney to prepare an amendment to the trust, naming a new beneficiary.

BANK AND SECURITIES ACCOUNTS ✍

If the decedent was a beneficiary of your bank or securities account, or if the decedent was a joint owner of your bank account or securities account, then it is important to contact the financial institution and tell them about the death. You may wish to arrange for a new beneficiary or joint owner at this time.

PENSION PLANS ✍

If the decedent was a beneficiary under your pension plan, then you need to notify them of his death and name a new beneficiary. Many pension plans require that you notify them within a set period of time (usually 30 days) so it is important to notify them as soon as you are able. If the decedent was a beneficiary of your Individual Retirement Account ("IRA") or of your Qualified Retirement Plan ("QRP") and you did not provide for an alternate beneficiary, then you need to name someone at this time.

There are many government regulations relating to IRA and QRP accounts. For example, you must begin to withdraw money from the account on April 1st of the year after you reach the age of 70 1/2. How much you must withdraw depends on whether you choose to base the amount withdrawn on your own life expectancy or on the joint life expectancy of you and your oldest beneficiary. If you have not reached the age of 70 1/2, then before naming a new beneficiary, you may wish to consult with your accountant or estate planning attorney to decide which is the best option for you.

NOTIFYING CREDITORS

If a probate procedure is necessary, and the decedent owed money, then it is the job of the person appointed as Personal Representative to determine whether the creditor needs to be notified of the death. If the Personal Representative finds that a creditor should be given notice, then it is his job to do so. The attorney who handles the probate will explain to the Personal Representative how notice is to be given.

If no probate procedure is necessary, then the next of kin can notify the creditors of the death, but before doing so, read Chapter 4: WHAT BILLS NEED TO BE PAID? That chapter explains what bills need to be paid and who is responsible to pay them.

Before any bill can be paid you need to know whether the decedent left any assets that could be used to pay those debts. The next chapter explains how to identify, and then locate all of the property owned by the decedent.

Locating the Assets 3

It is important to locate the financial records of the decedent and then carefully examine those records. Even the partner of a long-term marriage should conduct a thorough search because the surviving spouse may be unaware of all that was owned (or owed) by the decedent.

It is not unusual for a surviving spouse to be surprised when learning of the decedent's business transactions — especially in those cases where the decedent had control of family finances. One such example is that of Sam and Helen. They married just as soon as Sam was discharged from the army after World War II. During their marriage, Sam handled all of the finances, giving Helen just enough money to run the household.

Every now and again Helen would think of getting a job. She longed to have her own source of income and some economic independence. Each time she brought up the subject Sam would loudly object. He had no patience for this new "woman's lib" thing. Sam said he got married to have a real wife — one who would cook his meals and keep house for him.

Helen was not the arguing type. She rationalized, saying that Sam had a delicate stomach and dust allergies. He needed her to prepare his special meals and keep an immaculate house for him. Besides, Sam had a good job with a major cruise line and he needed her to accompany him on his frequent business trips.

Once Sam retired, he was even more cautious in his spending habits. Helen seldom complained. She assumed the reason for his "thrift" was that they had little money and had to live on his pension.

They were married 52 years when Sam died at the age of 83. Helen was 81 at the time of his death. She was one very happy, very angry and very aged widow when she discovered that Sam left her with assets worth well over a million dollars!

LOCATING FINANCIAL RECORDS

To locate the decedent's assets you need to find evidence of what he owned and where those assets are located. His financial records should lead you to the location of all of his assets so your first job is to locate those records. The best place to start the search is in the decedent's home. Many people keep their financial records in a single place but it is important to check the entire house to be sure you did not miss something.

CHECK THE COMPUTER
Don't overlook that computer sitting silently in the corner. It may hold the decedent's check register and all of the decedent's financial records. The computer may be programmed to protect information. If you cannot access the decedent's records, you may need to employ a computer technician or computer consultant who will be able to print out all of the information on the hard drive of the computer. You can find such a technician or consultant by looking in the telephone book under
COMPUTER SUPPORT SERVICES   or
COMPUTER SYSTEM DESIGNS & CONSULTANTS.

COLLECT AND IDENTIFY KEYS

The decedent may have kept his records in a safe deposit box, so you may find that your first job is to locate the keys to the box. As you go through the personal effects of the decedent, collect and identify all the keys that you find. If you come across an unidentified key, it could be a key to a post office box (private or federal) or a safe deposit box located in a bank or in a private vault company. You will need to determine whether that key opens a box that contains property belonging to the decedent or whether the key is to a box no longer in use. Some ways to investigate are as follows:

☑ CHECK BUSINESS RECORDS

If the decedent kept receipts, look through those items to see if he paid for the rental of a post office or safe deposit box. Also, check his check register to see if he wrote out a check to the Postmaster or to any safe deposit or vault company. Look at his bank statements to see if there is any bank charge for a safe deposit box. Some banks bill separately for safe deposit boxes so check with all of the banks in which the decedent had an account to determine if he had a box with that bank.

☑ CHECK THE KEY TYPE

If you cannot identify the key take the key to all of the local locksmiths and ask whether anyone can identify the type of facility that uses such keys. If that doesn't work then go to each bank, post office and private safe deposit boxes located in places where the decedent shopped, worked or frequented and ask whether they use the type of key that you found.

☑ CHECK THE MAIL

Check the mail over the next several months to see if the decedent receives a statement requesting payment for the next year's rental of a post office or safe deposit box.

You may find evidence of a brokerage account, bank account, or safe deposit box by examining correspondence addressed to the decedent. If the decedent was living alone, then have the mail forwarded to the person he named as Personal Representative or Executor of his Will. If the decedent did not leave a Will then the mail should be forwarded to his next of kin. Call the Postmaster and ask him/her to send you the necessary forms to make the change. Request that the mail be forwarded for the longest period allowed by law (currently one year).

The decedent may have been renting a post office box at his local post office branch or perhaps at the branch closest to where he did his banking. Ask the Postmaster to help you determine whether the decedent was renting a post office box. If so, then you need to locate the key to the box so that you can collect the decedent's mail.

 Special Situation LOST POST OFFICE BOX KEY

If the decedent had a post office box and you cannot locate the key, then contact the local postmaster and ask him/her what documentation is needed for you to gain possession of the mail in that box. As before, you will ask the Postmaster to have all future mail addressed to that box, forwarded to the Personal Representative, or if there is no Will, then to the decedent's next of kin.

WHAT TO DO WITH CHECKS

You may receive checks in the mail made out to the decedent. Social security checks, pension checks and annuity checks issued after the date of death need to be returned to the sender (see pages 30 and 32). Other checks need to be deposited to the decedent's bank account. The decedent is not here to endorse the check, but you can deposit to his account by writing his bank account number on the back of the check and printing beneath it "**FOR DEPOSIT ONLY.**" The bank will accept such an endorsement and deposit the check into the decedent's account. If the check is significant in value and/or the decedent had different accounts that are accessible to different people, then there needs to be cooperation and a sense of fair play. If not, the dollar gain may not nearly offset the emotional turmoil. Such was the case with Gail.

Gail's father made her a joint owner of his checking account to assist in paying his bills. He had macular degeneration and it was increasingly difficult for him to see. The father also had a savings account that was in his name only.

Gail's brother, Richard, had a good paying job in Canada. Even though he lived at a distance, Richard, his wife and two children always spent the Christmas break with his father. Gail's good cooking added to the festivities.

Summers were still another time for a visit with Richard and his family. His father enjoyed leaving the heat of North Carolina to spend a few weeks with Richard. One August, his father purchased a round trip ticket to Canada. It cost several hundred dollars. Before the departure date, his father had a heart attack and died.

Gail called the airline to cancel the ticket. They refunded the money in a check made out to her father. She deposited the check into the joint account.

As part of the probate procedure, the money in the father's savings account was divided equally between Richard and his sister. Richard wondered what happened to the money from the airline tickets. Gail explained "He paid for the tickets from the joint account, so I deposited the money back to the joint account. "

"Well aren't you going to give me half?"

"Dad meant for me to have whatever was in that joint account. If he wanted you to have half of the money, he would have made you joint owner as well."

Richard didn't see it that way:
"That refund was part of Dad's Probate Estate. It should have been deposited to his savings account to be divided equally between us. Are you going force me to argue this in court?"

Gail finally agreed to split the money with Richard, but the damage was done.

Gail complains that holidays are lonely since Dad died.

LOCATE OUT OF STATE ACCOUNTS
If the decedent had out of state bank or brokerage accounts, then you might be able to locate them if they mail the decedent monthly or quarterly statements. Not all institutions do so, but all institutions are required to send out an IRS tax form 1099 each year giving the amount of interest earned on that account. Once those forms come in, you will learn the location of all of the decedent's active accounts.

COLLECT LEGAL DOCUMENTS

As you go through the papers of the decedent you may come across documents that indicate property ownership, such as bank registers, title to motor vehicles, stock or bond certificates, insurance policies, brokerage account statements, etc. Place all evidence of ownership in a single place. You will need to contact different institutions to transfer title to the proper beneficiary. Chapter 5 explains how to identify the proper beneficiary. Chapter 6 explains how to transfer the property to that beneficiary.

LOCATING TITLE TO THE MOTOR VEHICLE

In North Carolina, if monies are owed on a car, then the lender takes possession of the certificate of title until the loan is paid. If you cannot find the original certificate of title, then it is either lost or monies are owed on the car and the lienholder has the title. To get information you can go to the local License Plate Office (tag agent) or you can write to: DMV's Vehicle Registration Section
    1100 New Bern Avenue; Raleigh, NC 27697
They charge $10 for a duplicate title. You may first want to call them at (919) 715-7000 to find out what information and documentation they may require. If you find there is a lien on the car then contact the lienholder and get a copy of the contract that is the basis of the loan. You may find that the car is leased and not owned by the decedent. If so, contact the lessor and get a copy of the lease agreement. Once you have the contract, check to see whether the decedent had life insurance as part of the agreement. If he did, then the lease is now paid in full. The Personal Representative or next of kin can send the death certificate to the leasing company with a copy of the contract and a letter requesting that the paid contract be transferred to the beneficiary who can use the car for the remainder of the leasing period, or take title to the car, whichever option is available under the lease agreement.

COLLECT DEEDS

Collect the deeds to all property owned by the decedent. Many people keep deeds in a safe deposit box. If you cannot find the deed in the decedent's home, then you need to determine whether he had a safe deposit box. (See the end of this Chapter for information about how to get into the safe deposit box.)

If you know that the decedent owned real property (lot, residence, condominium, cooperative, time share, etc.) but you cannot locate the deed, then contact the county recorder, in the county in which the property is located, and ask for a copy of the deed. You will need to identify the parcel of land by giving the legal description of the land or its parcel identification number. You can find this information on the last tax bill sent to the decedent. If you cannot find the last tax bill, then call the County Tax Collector or Tax Assessor for the information.

You can use the same procedure if you cannot locate the deed to property owned by the decedent in another state, namely, check with the recording department in the county where the property is located. Many states keep their land records in the court house. You can call the Clerk of the Circuit Court for information. In other states there is a separate recording department and you may need to contact the County Recorder or Registrar of Deeds.

THE DECEDENT'S RESIDENTIAL LEASE

If the decedent was renting his residence, then he may have a written lease agreement. It is important to locate the lease because the decedent's estate may be responsible for payments under the lease. If you cannot locate the lease, then ask the landlord for a copy. If the landlord reports that there was no written lease, then verify that the decedent was on a month to month basis and then work out a mutually agreeable time in which to vacate the premises.

If a written lease is in effect, then determine the end of the lease period, and whether there was a security deposit. Ask whether the landlord will agree to cancel the lease on the condition that the property is left in good condition. If the landlord says that the estate is responsible to pay the balance of the lease, then it is prudent to have an attorney review the lease to determine what rights and responsibilities remain now that the tenant is deceased.

ONGOING BUSINESS

If the decedent was the sole owner of a business, or if he owned a partnership interest in a business, the Personal Representative needs to contact the company accountant to obtain the company's business records. If there is a company attorney, then the attorney may be able to assist in obtaining the records. If you are a beneficiary of the estate, consider consulting with your own attorney to determine what rights and responsibilities you may have in the business.

COLLECT TAX RECORDS

You will need to file the decedent's final state and federal income tax return so you need to collect all of his tax records for the past 3 years. If you cannot locate his prior tax records, then check his personal telephone book and/or his personal bank register to see if he employed an accountant. If you can locate his accountant, then contact the accountant to see if he/she has a copy of those records.

If you are unable to locate the decedent's federal tax returns then they can be obtained from the IRS. The IRS will send copies of the decedent's tax filings to anyone who has a *fiduciary relationship* with the decedent. The IRS considers the following people to be fiduciaries:

➤ the person named as Personal Representative (or Executor) of the decedent's Will
➤ the Successor Trustee of the decedent's trust
➤ if the person died without a Will, then whoever is legally entitled to possession of the decedent's property

See Chapter 5 to learn who are the beneficiaries.

To notify the IRS of the fiduciary capacity, you need to file Form 56: NOTICE CONCERNING FIDUCIARY RELATIONSHIP

To request the copies, file IRS Form 4506:
   REQUEST FOR COPY OR TRANSCRIPT OF TAX FORM
Your accountant can file these forms for you or you can obtain the forms from the IRS by calling (800) 829-3676 or you can download them from the Internet:

 IRS FORMS WEB SITE
http://www.irs.gov/forms_pubs/forms.html

STATE INCOME TAX RETURN

If you cannot locate the decedent's state income tax return you can obtain copies from the North Carolina Department of Revenue. The Department Of Revenue will provide a copy of the decedent's return to the spouse or anyone who has a Power of Attorney. If the copy of the return is requested by anyone else the Department may require that a Personal Representative be appointed by the probate court before they will forward a copy of the decedent's tax records.

You can fax your request to (919) 715-0397 or you can write to: North Carolina Department of Revenue
           Correspondence Unit; P.O. Box 1168
                Raleigh, NC 27602

You will probably save time if you first call the North Carolina Department of Revenue at (919) 733-4682 and ask what information they need in order to forward copies of the tax return to you.

FINDING LOST/ ABANDONED PROPERTY

If the decedent was forgetful, he may have money in a lost bank or securities account or abandoned safe deposit box. North Carolina law requires that if an account has been inactive for a period of time and the location of the owner of the property cannot be determined after a diligent search, then the property must be turned over to the State Treasurer. The period of time varies:

- ⏳ 2 years for contents of a safe deposit box
- ⏳ 5 years for a checking or savings account
- ⏳ 10 years from the maturity date of a CD
- ⏳ 5 years for unclaimed wages
- ⏳ 15 years for a traveler's check

(NCGS 53-43.7, 116B-12)

Each year the State Treasurer prepares a list of abandoned property and forwards that list to the Clerk of the Superior Court of each county. The Treasurer then publishes notice in a newspaper stating that anyone can inspect the list at the Clerk's office. If no one comes forward, tangible property is sold at public auction and the proceeds turned over to the State Treasurer. Anyone who later makes a valid claim for the property will receive the abandoned cash, or net proceeds of the sale, from the State Treasurer (NCGS 116B-38, 116B-62).

You can ask the Clerk of the Superior court whether the decedent left abandoned property or you call the State Treasurer at (919) 508-5979 or you can write to:

North Carolina Department of State Treasurer
Escheat and Unclaimed Property Program
325 North Salisbury Street
Raleigh, NC 27603

The Department of State Treasurer lists the names of persons who may have unclaimed property in the state at their Web site:

 NC DEPARTMENT OF STATE TREASURER
http://www.treasurer.state.nc.us/escheats/

CLAIMS FOR DECEDENT VICTIM OF HOLOCAUST
The New York State Banking Department has a special Claims Processing Office for Holocaust survivors or their heirs. The office processes claims for Swiss bank accounts that were dormant since the end of World War II. If the decedent was a victim of the Holocaust, you can get information about money that may be due to the decedent's estate by calling (800) 695-3318.

CLAIMS IN OTHER STATES
Each state has an agency or department that is responsible for handling lost, abandoned or unclaimed property located within that state. If the decedent had residences in other states, then call the UNCLAIMED or ABANDONED PROPERTY department to see if the decedent has unclaimed property in that state.

EAGLE PUBLISHING COMPANY OF BOCA lists telephone numbers for the unclaimed property division for each state at their Web site:

 EAGLE PUBLISHING COMPANY OF BOCA WEB SITE
http://www.eaglepublishing.com

LOCATE CONTRACTS

If the decedent belonged to a health club or gym, he may have prepaid for the year. Look for the club contract. It will give the terms of the agreement. If you cannot locate the contract then contact the company for a copy of the agreement. If the contract was prepaid, then determine whether the agreement provides for a refund for the unused portion.

SERVICE CONTRACT

Many people purchase appliance service contracts to have their appliances serviced in the event that an appliance should need repair. If the decedent had a security system then he may have had a service contract with a company to monitor the system and contact the police in the event of a break-in.

If the decedent had a service contract, then you need to locate it and determine whether it can be assigned to the new owner of the property. If the contract is assignable, the new owner can reimburse the decedent's estate for the unused portion. If the contract cannot be assigned, then once the property is transferred, try to obtain a refund for the unused portion of the contract.

LOCATE OUT OF STATE ACCOUNTS

If the decedent had out of state bank or brokerage accounts, then you might be able to locate them if they mail the decedent monthly or quarterly statements. Not all institutions do so, but all institutions are required to send out an IRS tax form 1099 each year giving the amount of interest earned on that account. Once those forms come in, you will learn the location of all of the decedent's active accounts.

FILING THE WILL

If you have the original of the decedent's Will, and a probate procedure is necessary, then you need to file the Will with the Clerk of the Superior court in the county of North Carolina where the decedent resided. There is only one original Will, so it is important to hand carry the original document to the Clerk. If you are unable to make the delivery in person, you can mail the Will to the Clerk, but send it by registered mail so that you will have proof of delivery. Make a copy of the Will for your own records before delivering it to the Clerk.

WILL DRAFTED IN ANOTHER STATE OR COUNTRY

The state of North Carolina respects the laws of other states and countries. If a Will is drafted in another state or country, then it can be admitted for Probate in the state of North Carolina (NCGS 21-12).

If the Will is written in a foreign language, then it must be accompanied by a true and complete English translation before it can be admitted to Probate.

 **LAWYER**

OUT OF STATE PROPERTY OR RESIDENCE

If the decedent had his residence in North Carolina, and owned property in another state, then North Carolina law requires that the original (initial) probate procedure be conducted in this state (NCGS 28A-26-1). It may be necessary to have an *ancillary* (secondary) probate procedure in the state where the decedent's property is located.

If the decedent had his residence in another state and owned property in North Carolina, then you may need to have an initial probate procedure in that state and an ancilliary probate in North Carolina. Many state have laws that determine the location of the original administration, so it may be that you have no choice in the matter. In other states however, the choice of state is up to the Personal Representative.

If the decedent owned property in more than one state, the before depositing the Will with the court, then you need to determine where the original administration is to be held. To make that determination you need to consult with an attorney in each state who is experienced in probate matters.

Each state has its own probate statutes and tax structure. If you have a choice of location for the original administration, then ask each attorney whether the location of the initial probate procedure will have any effect on the total cost of the probate procedure, or who is to inherit the property, or how much the estate will be taxed.

LOCATING THE WILL

Most people put off making a Will until they think they need to. For most people that need arises when they are elderly and/or seriously ill and have assets that they want to leave to someone. If the decedent was relatively young, with few assets, and you cannot find a Will, then he probably died without one.

Those who make a Will, usually tell the person that they appoint as Executor, of the existence of the Will. Chances are, that someone in the decedent's circle of family and friends, knows whether or not there is a Will. If you don't come across a Will, then check to see if the decedent told anyone about having a Will. If you believe that the decedent had a Will, but you cannot find it, then there are at least three places to check out:

⇨ **THE CLERK OF THE SUPERIOR COURT**
North Carolina law gives residents the right to deposit their Will with the Clerk of the Superior Court in the county of their residence. If the decedent lived in other counties during his lifetime, then you need to check with the Clerk in each of those counties (NCGS 31-11).

⇨ **THE DECEDENT'S SAFE DEPOSIT BOX**
If you believe that the decedent had a Will but you cannot find it, then check to see if the decedent had a safe deposit box. If he did, you will need to gain entry to that box to see whether the Will is in the box. See page 75 for an explanation of how to gain entry to the safe deposit box.

⇨ THE DECEDENT'S ATTORNEY

Look at the decedent's checkbook for the past few years and see whether he paid any attorney fees. If you are able to locate the decedent's attorney, then call and inquire whether the attorney ever drafted a Will for the decedent, and if so, whether the attorney has the original Will in his possession. If the attorney has the original Will, then ask the attorney to forward the Will to the Clerk of the Superior court. Asking the attorney to forward the Will to the court does not obligate you to employ the attorney should you later find that a probate procedure is necessary.

 **A COPY AND NO ORIGINAL**

If you have a copy of the Will but cannot locate the original then the court will allow the estate of the decedent to be probated using the copy, provided you can prove that the document is a true copy of the decedent's valid, unrevoked Will (NCGS 98-4, 98-6).

You will need to employ an attorney who is experienced in probate matters to present such proof to the court.

ACCESSING THE SAFE DEPOSIT BOX

If the decedent had access to a safe deposit box, either as the lessee of the box, or even as a co-tenant of the box, then as soon as the bank (or the institution leasing the box, the "Lessor") learns of the death they will lock the box. The Lessor will allow a co-tenant of the safe deposit box to enter the safe deposit box, however they will require the co-tenant take an inventory of the contents of the box and give a copy of the inventory to the Lessor.

If the decedent was the only one with access to the safe deposit box, then someone will need to be appointed as Personal Representative in order to get the contents of the box. Once the Personal Representative presents his Letters to the Lessor he will be allowed access to the box. Again, North Carolina law requires that an inventory of the box be taken and a copy of the inventory given to the Lessor.

But suppose you do not know if a probate procedure is necessary, or even whether there is anything of value in the box? In such case, if you have the key to the decedent's safe deposit box, you can go to the Clerk of the Superior Court in the county where the box is located, and ask the Clerk to assist you in gaining access to the box to examine its contents. The Clerk will accompany you to the box. The Clerk will take an inventory of the box and give you, the Secretary of Revenue and the Lessor a copy of that inventory. If the Will is in the box, the Clerk will file it in the Superior Court. Nothing else can be removed until a Personal Representative is appointed (NCGS 28A-15-13). If you need to gain entry to the safe deposit box, you might save time if you first call the Clerk and ask what is needed for the procedure.

What Bills Need To Be Paid?   4

North Carolina is a state that respects the rights of creditors. If the estate of the decedent has sufficient assets, then the Personal Representative of the decedent's estate has the duty to be sure that all of the decedent's valid bills are paid. If the decedent had many debts, there may not be sufficient funds to pay all of the bills. The only remaining question is whether anyone else is responsible to pay those bills. If the decedent was married, then the first person the debtor will look to, is the decedent's spouse.

Historically, a husband was legally held responsible for his wife's debts, in particular if those debts were for her basic necessities (food, clothing, shelter). We inherited our legal system from England. Under the old English common law, once a woman married, her legal identity merged with that of her husband. A married woman had no right to own property or to enter into a contract in her own name. Once married, a woman became totally dependent on her husband and he was legally responsible to provide her with basic necessities including medical services. If anyone provided these necessities to his wife, then regardless of whether the husband agreed to be responsible for the debt, he became obliged to pay for them. This law was called the DOCTRINE OF NECESSARIES.

In 1911, the state of North Carolina passed the Martin Act (now NCGS 52-2). That law essentially gave a married woman, in the state of North Carolina, the right to own property and to enter into a contract without her husband's permission. After the Married Women's Rights law was passed, a series of cases tested whether the Doctrine of Necessaries still applied in the state of North Carolina. Questions that judges had to decide were:

If a wife can own property and contract to pay for her own necessaries, should her husband be responsible for her debts, in the event that she does not have enough money to pay for them?

And if the husband is responsible for his wife's debts, should she be responsible for his?

Courts answered "yes" to both questions (*North Carolina Baptist Hospitals vs. Harris.*, 354 S.E.2d 471 (NC 1987)). In North Carolina, anyone who provides necessaries for a married person has the right to demand payment from the spouse — whether or not the supporting partner agreed to be personally liable to pay for those necessaries.

This right continues after death. If the decedent was married and owed money for necessaries then the creditor can demand payment from the decedent's estate. If there are not sufficient funds in the estate, then the creditor can look to the spouse to pay the debt.

In this chapter we discuss the responsibilities of the surviving spouse, as well as others who may be responsible to pay debts left by the decedent, beginning with joint debts.

JOINT DEBTS

A *joint debt* is a debt that two or more people are responsible to pay. Usually the contract or promissory note reads that both parties agree to *joint and several* liability, meaning they both agree to pay the debt and each of them, individually, agree to be pay the debt. A joint debt can also be in the form of monies owed by one person with payment guaranteed by another person. If the person who owes the money does not pay, then the *guarantor* is responsible to pay the debt.

Before paying a bill, determine whether it is the decedent's debt or a joint debt. Hospital bills, nursing home bills, funeral expenses, legal fees incurred because of the decedent's death are all debts of the decedent's estate. They are not joint debts unless someone guaranteed payment for the monies owed.

PAYING FOR THE JOINT DEBT

If another person is jointly responsible for monies owed by the decedent, then that bill should be paid from any joint account held with the decedent. If the joint debtor did not have a joint account with the decedent, then the joint debtor must pay the bill from his/her own funds.

| SPOUSE | DEBTS THE SPOUSE MUST PAY |

In addition to being responsible to pay for the decedent spouse's necessaries, the surviving spouse must pay for any of their joint debts. Loans signed by the decedent and his spouse are joint debts, as are charges on credit cards that both were authorized to use. Property taxes are a joint debt if the decedent and the spouse both owned the property.

JOINT PROPERTY BUT NO JOINT DEBT

Suppose all of the decedent's funds are held jointly with a family member and the joint owner of the account did not agree to pay those debts? Can the creditor require that the decedent's share of the joint funds be set aside to pay the debt?

The answer to this question depends on how the joint property is titled. As we will see in Chapter 5 there are different ways to hold property jointly with another. If the property is held jointly *with rights of survivorship*, then the surviving owner owns the property as of the date of death. If there is no right of survivorship, then the creditor has the right to demand that the decedent's share be used to pay his debt. This applies to joint bank accounts, or jointly held securities, or real property that the decedent held jointly with another.

Even with the right of survivorship, the decedent's share of joint property may be used to pay his bills. North Carolina statute gives the Personal Representative the right to require the decedent's share of the joint property be used to pay claims against the decedent's estate. The Personal Representative cannot require the decedent's share of the joint property be used to pay his bills unless a valid claim has been filed against the decedent's estate, and there are no other funds available to pay that claim (NCGS 28A-15-10, 41-2.2).

NO MONEY — NO PROPERTY

If the decedent owed money then the bill needs to be paid from assets owned by the decedent — which leads to the next question "Did the decedent have any money in his own name when he died?"

If the decedent died without any money or property in his name, then there is no money to pay any creditor. The only question that remains is whether anyone else is liable to pay those bills. The issue of payment most often arises in relation to services provided by nursing homes. When a person enters a nursing home, he is usually too ill to speak for himself or even sign his name. In such cases, the nursing home administrator will ask the spouse or a family member to sign a battery of papers on behalf of the patient before allowing the patient to enter the facility. Buried in that battery of papers may be a statement that the family member agrees to be responsible for payment to the nursing home. If the family member refuses to guarantee payment and the patient's finances are limited, then the facility may refuse to admit the patient.

If a nursing home accepts Medicare or Medicaid payments, then under the Federal Nursing Home Reform Law, that nursing home is prohibited from requiring a family member to guarantee payment as a condition of allowing the patient to enter that facility. USC Title 42 §1395I-3(c)(5)(A)(ii). Nonetheless, it is common practice for the nursing home, in effect, to say "Either someone agrees to pay for the patient's bill or you need to find a different facility."

Their position is understandable. Most nursing homes are business establishments and not charitable organizations. The nursing home must be paid for the services they provide or they soon will be out of business. For a patient without money, the solution to the problem is to have the patient admitted to a facility as a Medicaid patient.

But what if the decedent had some money when he entered the nursing home and you agreed to guarantee payment to the nursing home?

What if you feel that you were coerced into signing as a guarantor?

Are you now liable to pay the decedent's final nursing home bill if your family member died without funds?

An experienced Elder Law attorney will be able to answer these questions after examining the documents that you signed and the conditions under which the patient entered the nursing home.

PAYING THE DECEDENT'S BILLS

If the decedent owed money and he died owning property, belonging to him alone, such as a bank account, securities, or real property, then there may be money available to pay monies owed by the decedent. It is up to the decedent's Personal Representative to pay all valid debts, but to do so the Personal Representative first must gain possession of the decedent's assets. To gain possession of the decedent's assets, there will need to be some sort of probate procedure to determine who is entitled to the decedent's property.

Once the probate procedure begins, all of the decedent's creditors will be given an opportunity to come forward and produce evidence showing how much is owed. The Personal Representative needs to look over each unpaid invoice and decide whether it is a valid bill. The problem with making that decision is that the decedent is not here to say whether he actually received the goods and services now being billed to his estate.

That is especially the case for medical or nursing care bills. An example of improper billing brought to the attention of this author was that of a bill submitted for a physical examination of the decedent. The bill listed the date of the examination as July 10th, but the decedent died on July 9th. Other incorrect billings may not be as obvious, so each invoice needs to be carefully examined.

If the Personal Representative decides to challenge a bill, and is unable to settle the matter with the creditor, then the probate court will decide whether the debt is valid and should be paid.

MEDICAL BILLS COVERED BY INSURANCE

If the decedent had health insurance you may receive an invoice stamped "THIS IS NOT A BILL." This means the health care provider has submitted the bill to the decedent's health insurance company and expects to be paid by them. Even though payment is not requested, it is important that you verify that the bill is valid for two reasons:

➢ **LATER LIABILITY**

If the insurer refuses to pay the claim, the facility will seek payment from whoever is in possession of the decedent's property, and that may reduce the amount inherited by the beneficiaries.

➢ **INCREASED HEALTH CARE COSTS**

Regardless of whether the decedent was covered by a private health care insurer or Medicare, improper billing increases the cost of health insurance to all of us. Consumers pay high premiums for health coverage. We, as taxpayers, all share the cost of Medicare. If unnecessary or fraudulent billing is not checked, then ultimately, we all pay.

 *Special Situation*   MEDICARE FRAUD

If you believe that you have come across a case of Medicare fraud, you can call the ANTI-FRAUD HOTLINE (800)447-8477 and report the incident to the Office of the Inspector General of the United States Department of Health and Human Services.

HOW TO CHECK MEDICARE BILLING

If the decedent was covered by Medicare, then an important billing question is whether the health care provider agreed to accept Medicare *assignment of benefits*, meaning that they agreed to accept payment directly from Medicare. If so, the maximum liability for the patient is **20%** of the amount determined as reasonable by Medicare. For example, suppose a doctor bills Medicare $1,000 for medical treatment of the decedent. If Medicare determines that a reasonable fee is $800, then the patient is liable for 20% of the $800 ($160).

Health care providers who do not accept Medicare assignment bill the patient directly. They can charge up to 15% more than the amount allowed by Medicare. If the decedent knew and agreed to be liable for the payment, then his estate may be liable for whatever Medicare doesn't pay. For example, if a doctor's bill is $1,000 and Medicare allows $800, then Medicare will reimburse the decedent's estate 80% of $800 ($640). The doctor may charge the estate 15% more than the $800 ($920) and the estate may be liable for the difference: $920 - $640 or $280.

To summarize:
For health care providers accepting Medicare assignment, the most they can bill the decedent's estate is 20% of what Medicare allows (not 20% of what they bill.)

Those who do not accept Medicare assignment, can bill 15% more than the amount allowed by Medicare. The decedent's estate may be liable for the difference between the amount billed and the amount paid by Medicare.

In either case, if the decedent had secondary health care insurance, then the secondary insurer may be responsible to pay for the difference. If you have a question about Medicare billing call MEDICARE PART B CUSTOMER SERVICE (800) 333-7586.

| Special Situation | DENIAL OF MEDICARE COVERAGE |

If the health care provider reports to you that services provided to the decedent are not covered by Medicare, or if the facility submits the bill to Medicare and Medicare refuses to pay, then check to see if you agree with that ruling by determining what services are covered under Medicare. See page 49 to get publications on what is (or is not) covered. You can also call the toll free Medicare Hotline (800) 633-4227. English and Spanish speaking operators are available Monday through Friday from 8 a.m. to 4:30 p.m. For the hearing impaired call TTY/TDD call (877) 486-2048.

THE MEDICARE APPEAL

If you believe that the decedent has wrongly been denied coverage, then you can appeal that decision. North Carolina's Senior Health Insurance Information Program can give you information that may help you with your Medicare appeal. You can call them at (800) 443-9354. If you are calling from out of state, call (919) 733-0111.

You can also call the North Carolina Bar (800) 662-7660 for a referral to an attorney experienced in Medicare appeals. Some attorneys work *pro bono* (literally for the public good; i.e. without charge) but most charge to assist in an appeal. Federal statute 42 U.S.C. §406(a)(2)(A) limits the amount an attorney may charge for a successful Medicare appeal to 25% of the amount recovered or $4,000, whichever is the smaller amount.

SOME THINGS ARE CREDITOR PROOF

Sometimes it happens that the decedent had money or property titled in his name only, but he also had a significant amount of debt. In such cases the beneficiaries may wonder whether they should go through a probate procedure if there will be little, if anything, left after the creditors are paid. Before making the decision consider that some assets are protected under North Carolina law:

✧ THE HOMESTEAD ✧

North Carolina property owned and occupied by a person as his/her main residence is called *homestead* property. Should the owner of the homestead die, then Article X Section 4 (a) of the North Carolina Constitution protects the homestead from forced sale by the decedent's creditors. Specifically, if the decedent owned his home and he died with minor children, then no creditor can force the sale of the home until all his children reach the age of 18. If he has a spouse and no minor children, then none of his creditors can force the sale of that homestead while the spouse is living in the homestead. If the spouse remarries, or moves to another homestead, then the decedent's creditor protection is lost.

There are exceptions to this rule. Creditor protection does not extend to delinquent taxes or mortgages on the homestead or to mechanics' liens. For example, if there is a mortgage on the homestead and the surviving spouse does not make payments when due, then the lender has the right to foreclose on the house.

Of course, if the decedent was not married and had no minor children, then his homestead is not creditor proof.

✧ THE SPOUSE'S ALLOWANCE ✧

If the decedent had his principal residence in North Carolina and he was married at the time of his death, then his spouse is entitled to a spousal allowance of $10,000 for the support of the spouse for the year following the death. The spouse's allowance is exempt from the claims of any creditor. If the decedent left a Will, then the $10,000 is deducted from any gift that the spouse is to receive under the Will (NCGS 30-15).

✧ THE CHILD'S ALLOWANCE ✧

The decedent's children are entitled to an allowance of $2,000 for their support during the year following the death provided:

⇨ the child is under 18 — or —
⇨ the child is a full time student under 22 — or —
⇨ the child is totally disabled and under 21.

If the widow is pregnant at the time of the decedent's death, then her child is also entitled to a child's allowance.

If a child under 18, who is not the decedent's child, was living with the decedent (for example, a step-child), then that child may also be entitled to an allowance.

The child is entitled to the allowance <u>and</u> whatever share may have been left to the child under the Will, or under the Laws of Intestate Succession.

As with the Spouse's Allowance, the Child's Allowance is free from any claim made by a creditor of the decedent. (NCGA 30-17).

✧ INSURANCE AND PENSION PLANS ✧

A life insurance policy that is payable to a beneficiary, is not available to pay debts owed by the decedent. All of the proceeds of the policy will go directly to the beneficiary (NCGS 58-58-95, 58-58-115).

Any money held by the decedent in a Federal retirement plan 408 (IRA account) are exempt from creditor's claims. All monies received by beneficiaries of such plans are protected from the creditors of the decedent. (NCGS 1C-1601(a) (9)).

✧ MONIES FROM A WRONGFUL DEATH ACTION ✧

The Personal Representative can sue on behalf of the decedent for a wrongful or negligent act that caused the decedent's death. Usually such actions are taken on a contingency fee so that the attorney is not paid unless the suit is won. Hospital and medical expenses, burial expenses can be deducted from the award up to a maximum of 50% of the funds left after the payment of attorney fees and costs.

As part of the award, a family member may receive monies for loss of the decedent's income, companionship, or services. Anything left over after payment of attorney's fees, costs, expenses and special awards to family members are distributed to the next of kin as determined by the North Carolina Laws of Descent and Distribution (see Chapter 5). Monies received as a result of an award for a wrongful death are free from claims of the decedent's creditors (NCGS 28A-18-2).

✧ THERE IS A PRIORITY OF PAYMENT ✧

The next thing to consider is that not all probate debts are equal. North Carolina Statute 29A-19-6 establishes an order of priority for payment of claims made against the decedent's Probate Estate.

COST OF ADMINISTRATION

Top priority goes to the cost of the probate procedure including the fees charged by the Personal Representative and his attorney; and monies paid for the Spouse's Allowance and the Child's Allowance. All other claims are arranged by Class:

FIRST CLASS: SECURED CLAIMS

A secured claim is a claim that is backed by some item (usually a house or car) that the creditor can take should the debt be in default. Secured claims must be paid first but only up to the amount of the current value of the property; for example if a car is worth $10,000, but the loan value is $11,000, then the first $10,000 is a first class claim and the remaining $1,000 becomes a Seventh Class debt.

SECOND CLASS: FUNERAL EXPENSES

Second in priority is the decedent's funeral expenses, up to $2,500. This does not include the cemetery lot or headstone. Anything over $2,500 becomes a Seventh Class debt.

THIRD CLASS: FEDERAL TAXES

If there is a debt or a tax that has preference under Federal law, then it is a Class 3 debt.

FOURTH CLASS: NORTH CAROLINA TAXES

All dues, taxes, and other claims with preference under the laws of North Carolina are 4th in line for payment.

FIFTH CLASS: JUDGMENT LIENS

If the decedent had a judgment that was a lien against any of his property in the state of North Carolina, then that judgment is a Class 5 claim.

SIXTH CLASS: WAGES; MEDICAL BILLS

If the decedent employed workers, and owed them money for work done within a year of his death, then they are 6th in priority of payment. Claims for medical services and medical drugs or supplies for the care of the decedent up to a year prior to his death are also a sixth class claim.

SEVENTH CLASS: ALL OTHER CLAIMS

Claims against the decedent's Probate Estate must be paid in the above order. For example, suppose the decedent left enough money to pay for the probate, $2,500 of his funeral expenses with $10,000 left over. If there are no other debts then the beneficiaries get the $10,000.

Suppose instead that the decedent employed a housekeeper and owed her $5,000 for work done and he also owed $15,000 in hospital bills (both Class 6 claims). One quarter of the $20,000 in claims is owed to the housekeeper. Three quarters of the $20,000 debt is owed to the hospital. The remaining $10,000 is prorated in the same proportion, namely the housekeeper gets 1/4 of the $10,000 ($2,500) and the hospital gets the remaining $7,500. There is nothing left for the beneficiaries.

Medicaid is a program that provides medical and long term nursing care for people with low income and limited resources. The program is funded jointly by the federal and state government. Federal law 42 U.S.C. 1396(p) requires the state to recover monies spent from the estate of a Medicaid recipient who was 55 or older when the decedent received Medicaid assistance. The state will seek reimbursement for the cost of nursing home care or for homebased care or for other community based services. Under federal law, the state cannot recover Medicaid funds until the surviving spouse, and/or disabled child are deceased.

Even if the Medicaid recipient is single, there usually is no money to recover because to qualify for Medicaid in North Carolina, a person may not have more than $2,00 in assets.

Sometimes it happens that a person on Medicaid dies and his estate later receives money perhaps as part of a cash settlement of a lawsuit. In such case, the state of North Carolina will obtain a judgment lien and become a Class 5 creditor. This means that all the creditors in Class 1 through Class 4 have priority over any claim filed by the state of North Carolina against the estate of the decedent. Even fifth class creditors who have their judgments in force prior to the Medicaid lien have priority, meaning that those judgments must be paid prior to Medicaid reimbursement (NCGS 108A-70.5).

✧ THERE IS A STATUTE OF LIMITATIONS ✧

Finally, consider that there is a statute of limitations for bringing a claim against the Probate Estate of the decedent. The first job of the Personal Representative is to tell the decedent's creditors that the decedent died, and that a probate procedure is in progress. If the Personal Representative knows the identity of a creditor, then he must give the creditor notice by mail. The Personal Representative must publish notice in the newspaper for four successive weeks to inform any unknown creditor of the death. If a creditor fails to file a claim within three months after the date of the first publication (or the date the creditor receives written notice, then his claim is barred (NCGS 28A-14-1, 28A-19-3).

But what if no one starts a probate procedure?
North Carolina statute 28A-19-3(f) states that if a claim is not filed within three years from the date of death, then that claim cannot be enforced against the estate, the Personal Representative, or any of the beneficiaries.

There are exceptions to the three-year limit such as mortgages and federal claims and certain liens on the decedent's property. But, in general, if no one begins a probate procedure until three years have passed, then the beneficiaries may be able to obtain possession of the decedent's assets free from creditor claims.

Read on before you decide to wait out the three years.

DECEDENT LEAVING CONSIDERABLE DEBT

If the decedent died leaving much debt and no property, then the solution is simple. No probate, no one gets paid. But if the decedent had property and died owing a significant amount of money, his beneficiaries may be tempted to wait out the three year period and begin probate at that time. Such a strategy may turn out to be more hassle than its worth. Some creditors are tenacious and will use whatever legal strategy is available in order to be paid. For example, if no one starts a probate procedure, a creditor can petition the court to be appointed as Personal Representative of the estate (NCGS 28A-4-1 (b)).

Family members may object to having a creditor as a Personal Representative, so there could be a court battle over who has priority to be appointed as Personal Representative. There could be other disagreements regarding whether the claim is valid and should be paid. Court battles are expensive, emotionally as well as financially. Before you decide to wait out a creditor by postponing probate for three years, consult with an attorney experienced in probate matters for his/her opinion about the best way to administer the estate.

MONIES OWED TO THE DECEDENT

Suppose you owed money to the decedent? Do you need to pay that debt now that he is dead? That depends on whether there is some written document that says the debt is forgiven once the decedent dies. For example, suppose the decedent lent you money to buy your home. If he left a Will saying that once he dies, your debt is forgiven, then you do not need to make any more payments. If you signed a promissory note and mortgage at the time you borrowed the money from the decedent, then the Personal Representative should sign the original promissory note "PAID IN FULL" and return the note to you. If the mortgage was recorded, then the Personal Representative should sign and record a satisfaction of mortgage.

If you owed the decedent money and there is no Will, or if there is a Will, no mention of forgiving the debt, then you still owe the money. If you borrowed the money from the decedent and his spouse, then you need to pay the debt to the spouse. If you borrowed the money from the decedent only, then the debt becomes an asset to the estate of the decedent, meaning that you now owe the money to the decedent's beneficiaries. If you are one of those beneficiaries, you can deduct the money from your inheritance.

For example, suppose your father left $70,000 in a bank account to be divided equally between you and your two brothers. If you owed your father $20,000, then your father's estate is really worth $90,000. Instead of paying the $20,000, you can agree to receive $10,000 and have the $20,000 debt forgiven. Each of your brothers will then receive $30,000 in cash.

Who Are The Beneficiaries? 5

A question that comes up early on is who is entitled to the property of the decedent. To answer the question you first need to know how the property was titled (owned) as of the date of death.

There are three ways to own property. The decedent could have owned property jointly with another person; or in trust for another person; or the decedent could have owned property that was titled in his name only.

In general, upon the decedent's death:

> **Joint Property with rights of survivorship** belongs to the surviving joint owner.
>
> **Trust Property** belongs to the beneficiary of the trust.
>
> Property owned by the **decedent only** belongs to the beneficiaries named in the Will.
> If no Will, then the property goes to his heirs as per the North Carolina Laws of Descent and Distribution.
>
> **NOTE** ⇨ If the decedent was married, then his spouse may have rights in his property.

This chapter explains each of these types of ownership in detail.

PROPERTY HELD JOINTLY

Bank accounts, securities, motor vehicles, real property can all be owned jointly by two or more people. If one of the joint owners dies, then the survivor(s) continue to own their share of the property. Who owns the share belonging to the decedent depends on how the joint ownership was set up.

THE JOINT BANK ACCOUNT

If a bank account is opened in two or more names, then each depositor is given a statement of the terms and conditions of the account. The statement will say whether each depositor has authority to make a withdrawal, or whether two signatures are necessary. The statement will also say whether there are rights of survivorship. Unless the statement says there are rights of survivorship, none is presumed. Specifically, if the account does not say that the owners have a right of survivorship, then the account is a *Tenancy-in-Common* and the decedent's share of the account will go to the beneficiaries of the decedent's estate. It is presumed that the decedent had an equal share with the surviving owners of the account, unless the surviving owners can prove that the decedent contributed less (or more) than his equal share (NCGS 41-2.1).

If the surviving joint owner has the ability to withdraw funds on his own signature, then he can do so even if the other owner is deceased (NCGS 53-146). Once the bank learns of the death of a joint owner, then under North Carolina law, the bank must pay the decedent's share of the account to the Personal Representative. If there are sufficient funds in the Estate to pay the all of the claims against the Estate, then the Personal Representative will return the money to the joint owner (NCGS 41-2.1 (b)(4)).

If the surviving joint owner closes that account before the bank learns of the death, then the Personal Representative may later require that the surviving joint owner pay as much of the decedent's share as is necessary to pay the decedent's debts.

JOINTLY HELD SECURITIES

You can determine whether the decedent owns a security alone or jointly with another by examining the face of the stock or bond certificate. If two names are printed on the certificate followed by a statement that the owners are "joint owners with rights of survivorship," or the initials "JTWRS" then the surviving owner can either cash in the security or ask the company to issue a new certificate in the name of the surviving owner. As with the bank account, the Personal Representative has the right to ask that the decedent's share of the security be used to pay the decedent's bills if there are no other funds available (NCGS 41-2.2).

If the security does not say "with rights of survivorship," then you need to contact the company to determine how the account was set up; i.e. as a Tenancy-in-Common or survivorship rights. The same applies to securities held in a brokerage account. Not all brokerage firms print the name of a joint owner on the brokerage statement so even if the account appears to be in the decedent's name only, it is prudent to contact the brokerage firm and request a copy of the contract that is the basis of the account. The contract will show when the account was opened and the terms of the brokerage account. If you determine that the account is held jointly with rights of survivorship or for the benefit of someone, then have the brokerage firm forward the necessary forms to make the transfer to the proper owner or beneficiary.

JOINTLY HELD MOTOR VEHICLES

If a motor vehicle is held jointly, the name of each owner is printed on the title to the motor vehicle. If the title says that they are joint owners **with rights of survivorship,** then if one person dies, the survivor owns the car, 100%. If you are such surviving joint owner then you need to go to your local License Plate Office or Tag Agent to change title and registration. You can get a complete list of offices and Tag Agents from the Internet:

 DEPARTMENT OF MOTOR VEHICLE WEB SITE
http://www.dmv.dot.state.nc.us/

You may wish to first call to determine how much it will cost and what documents you will need to take with you (919) 715-7000.

It is important to change title as soon as you are able. You might be able to get a reduced insurance rate if there is only one person insured under the policy. Also, should the surviving owner be involved in an accident, and title has officially been changed, then it is clear that the estate of the decedent is in no way liable for the accident.

If title to the car was held jointly and there are no rights of survivorship, then the decedent's share of the car goes to his estate in the same manner as a motor vehicle held in the decedent's name only. This is true even if the decedent held the car jointly with the surviving spouse.

MOTOR VEHICLE IN DECEDENT'S NAME ONLY
If the decedent left a Will, then the car goes to the beneficiaries named in the Will. If the decedent died without a Will then the car goes to the decedent's heirs as defined in the North Carolina Laws of Descent and Distribution. We discuss these laws later in this chapter. See Chapter 6 for an explanation of how to transfer title to the motor vehicle.

NORTH CAROLINA REAL PROPERTY HELD JOINTLY

The name of the owner of real property is printed on the face of the deed. To determine whether the decedent owned the property jointly with another person, you need to look at the last recorded deed. See page 62 if you cannot locate the deed.

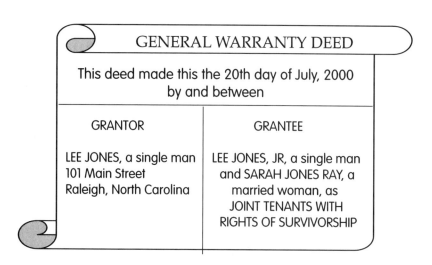

GENERAL WARRANTY DEED	
This deed made this the 20th day of July, 2000 by and between	
GRANTOR	GRANTEE
LEE JONES, a single man 101 Main Street Raleigh, North Carolina	LEE JONES, JR, a single man and SARAH JONES RAY, a married woman, as JOINT TENANTS WITH RIGHTS OF SURVIVORSHIP

In the above example, the **Grantor** of the deed (Lee Jones) transferred the property to his children Lee and Sarah. The children are the **Grantees** of the deed and now own the property. The property was transferred to them as joint tenants with rights of survivorship. Should one of the joint tenants die, then the surviving joint tenant will own the property 100% (NCGS 41-2). Nothing need be done to establish that ownership, however the decedent's name remains on the deed. As explained on page 24, the Register of Deeds in the county of the decedent's residence will keep a record of the death certificate so anyone examining title to the property will know that the joint tenant is deceased. If the property is located in another county, then you need to send the death certificate to the Register of Deeds in that county for recording.

📃 DEED HELD AS TENANTS IN COMMON

If the Grantee of a deed identifies the decedent and another as TENANTS IN COMMON then the decedent's share belongs to whomever the decedent named as his beneficiary in his Will. If the decedent died without a Will, then the North Carolina Laws of Descent and Distribution determine who inherits the property. See page 108 for an explanation of the law. If the deed named the decedent as a "Joint Tenant" with no mention of "Rights of Survivorship" then this is the same as a Tenancy in Common (NCGS 41-2).

If the decedent owned property as a Tenant In Common, then a probate procedure is necessary in order to transfer the decedent's share of the property to the proper beneficiary.

 LAWYER   THE AMBIGUOUS DEED

Some deeds do not clearly express the Grantor's intent. For example, if a deed is granted to: "Jay Simms and Dale Belham, jointly or to their survivor" could be read two ways. It could mean that the there are rights of survivorship or it could mean, that if one dies, his share goes to his survivor (i.e. a Tenancy in Common).

If the deed is not clear or is ambiguous, then a court hearing will need to be held to determine who inherits the property. The court will take evidence to determine the intent of the Grantor and will rule based on that evidence (NCGS 39-1.1)

▤ DEED WITH A LIFE ESTATE

A *Life Estate* interest in real property means that the person who owns the life estate has the right to live in that property until he/she dies. You can identify a life estate interest by examining the face of the deed. If somewhere on the face of the deed you see the phrase LIFE ESTATE WITH REMAINDER OVER or RESERVING A LIFE ESTATE to the decedent, then the Grantee(s) now own the property. For example, suppose the granting paragraph of the deed reads:

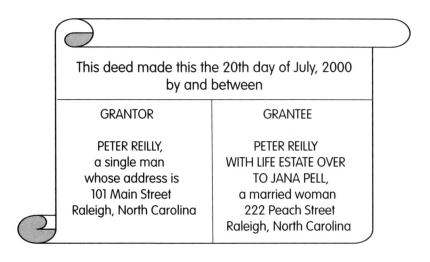

This deed made this the 20th day of July, 2000 by and between

GRANTOR	GRANTEE
PETER REILLY, a single man whose address is 101 Main Street Raleigh, North Carolina	PETER REILLY WITH LIFE ESTATE OVER TO JANA PELL, a married woman 222 Peach Street Raleigh, North Carolina

Peter Reilly is the owner of the Life Estate. While he is alive Jana Pell has no right to occupy the property. Once Peter dies, Jane owns the property, and is free to take possession of the property or transfer it, as she sees fit. As with a survivorship tenancy, nothing need be done to establish Jana's ownership of the property. If the property is located in the county of the decedent's residence then the County Register of Deeds will keep a record of the death certificate. If the property is in another county, then you need to forward the death certificate to the Register of Deeds in that county.

▤ DEED HELD AS HUSBAND AND WIFE

If the Grantee on the deed is identified as a married couple, for example: TODD AMES AND SUSAN AMES, H/W or
TODD AMES AND SUSAN AMES, HIS WIFE or
TODD AMES AND SUSAN AMES, HUSBAND AND WIFE
then this creates a *Tenancy by Entirety*. A Tenancy by Entirety is much the same as a Joint Tenancy with rights of survivorship. When one spouse dies, and providing they are married at the time of death, the surviving spouse owns the property 100% (NCGS 39-13.6).

The decedent's name remains on the deed. As with a life estate or survivorship tenancy, the Register of Deeds in the county where the property is located needs to be given a certified copy of the death certificate. If the property is located in the county of the decedent's residence, then the local Registrar will send the certificate to the Register of Deeds. If the property is in another county, then you need to forward a certified copy of the death certificate to the Register of Deeds and ask the Register to have the certificate recorded in that county.

MOBILE HOME OWNED AS HUSBAND AND WIFE
A mobile home is a motor vehicle, however if a married couple become co-owners of the mobile home, then unless the title says differently, the couple own the property as Tenants-by-the-Entirety. This means that each has rights of survivorship in that mobile home (NCGS 41-2.5).

If the land on which the mobile home is located is owned by the couple as husband and wife, then the surviving spouse owns that real property as well.

| ☎ LAWYER | OUT OF STATE PROPERTY |

This chapter relates only to property owned by the decedent in the State of North Carolina. If the decedent owned property in another state or country, then the laws of that state or country determine who inherits that property. You need to consult with an attorney in that state to determine who owns the property now that the Grantee is dead.

 THE INVALID DEED

The above discussion on the different types of ownership of real property presumes that you are in possession of the most recent, valid deed. It may be that there is a deed that was signed at a later time. For example, if the decedent divorced just before he died, then the Final Judgment of Divorce should say how property owned by the couple is to be divided. If you have a deed that states the property is held by the decedent as a Tenancy by the Entirety (i.e. as husband and wife), then there is probably a later deed that reflects that division of property.

Before you come to a conclusion about who inherits the property it is advisable to have an attorney do a title search to determine the owner of the property as of the decedent's date of death.

PROPERTY HELD IN TRUST

BANK/ SECURITY ACCOUNTS

If the decedent held a bank account or security account in his name "in trust for" or "for the benefit of" someone, then once the bank has a certified copy of the death certificate, the bank will turn over the account to the beneficiary. As with the joint account, if the Personal Representative does not have sufficient estate funds to pay the decedent's debts, then the Personal Representative can claim as much money from this account as he needs to pay those debts (NCGS 53-146.2).

If the bank or security account is registered in the name of the decedent "as Trustee under a Trust Agreement," that means the decedent was the Trustee of a Trust and the bank will turn over that account to the Successor Trustee of the trust. Banks usually require a copy of the trust when the account was opened, so the bank probably knows the identity of the Successor Trustee. If the trust was amended to name a different Successor Trustee, then he/she needs to present the bank with a copy of that amendment together with a certified copy of the death certificate. Whether the monies in the account can be used to pay the decedent's debts depends on the nature of the Trust Agreement. If the Trust was an Inter Vivos or Revocable Living Trust, then the funds are available to pay the decedent's debts.

MOTOR VEHICLE

If the motor vehicle is held in the name of the decedent "as trustee," then the motor vehicle is part of the trust property. The motor vehicle remains in the trust once the decedent trustee dies. The Successor Trustee will need to contact the motor vehicle bureau to have title changed to that of the Successor Trustee. Chapter 6 explains how to transfer title to the car.

REAL PROPERTY

If the decedent had a trust and put property that he owned in the trust then the deed may read something like this:

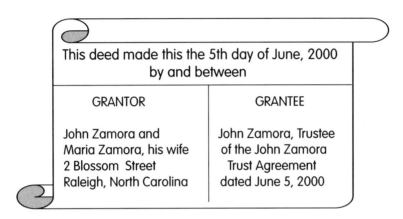

This deed made this the 5th day of June, 2000 by and between	
GRANTOR	GRANTEE
John Zamora and Maria Zamora, his wife 2 Blossom Street Raleigh, North Carolina	John Zamora, Trustee of the John Zamora Trust Agreement dated June 5, 2000

Once the trustee (John Zamora) dies then that property remains in the trust. The trust document will say whether the person who takes John's place as trustee (the Successor Trustee) should sell or keep the property or perhaps give it to a beneficiary. If no instruction is given, then what the Successor Trustee does with the property may be affected by laws relating to the administration of trust property in the state where the property is located. If you are a beneficiary of the trust and you are concerned about what the Successor Trustee will do with the property, then it is best to consult with your attorney.

NORTH CAROLINA DEED OF TRUST

The North Carolina Deed of Trust is very different from the above described deed. The Deed of Trust is essentially a mortgage. The owner of the property places title to the property with a Trustee as security for payment of monies owed to the lender. If the debt is not paid, then the Trustee (after proper foreclosure on the property) will deliver title to the property to the Beneficiary of the Deed of Trust, namely the lender.

PROPERTY IN DECEDENT'S NAME ONLY

If the decedent owned property that was in his name only (not jointly with rights of survivorship, or in trust for someone), then a probate procedure will be necessary before the heirs can get possession of that property. Who is entitled to the decedent's Probate Estate depends on whether the decedent died with or without a Will. If the decedent died testate, then the beneficiaries of the decedent's property are identified in the Will.

If the decedent died without a Will, then the state of North Carolina provides a Will for him in the form of a set of *Laws of Descent and Distribution* (also referred to as the *Intestate Succession Act)*. These laws determine who inherits the decedent's intestate probate estate and what percentage of the probate estate each heir is to receive once all the bills and costs of administering the probate procedure are paid.

The law recognizes the right of the family to inherit the decedent's property. The law covers all possible relationships beginning with the decedent's spouse.

WHAT'S A SPOUSE?

In this era of people challenging the concept of the family unit, those of a philosophical bent may ponder the meaning of marriage. Is it a union of two people in the eyes of God? Is it even a union? Maybe it is just a contract between two people. The state does not concern itself with such things. If a person dies without a Will, then the state will distribute the decedent's property according to the laws of the state; and the laws of the state determine whether two people are married.

MARRIED IN NORTH CAROLINA

To be married in North Carolina means that a man and a woman have obtained a license to marry from the state, solemnized the marriage by a state or religious ceremony, and then cohabited together as man and wife. North Carolina law specifically prohibits the marriage of people:

☒   who are related closer than first cousin

☒   who are currently married to another person

☒   either of whom are physically impotent

☒   either of whom lack sufficient understanding to enter into a marriage agreement.

Parental consent to marry is required for anyone between the ages of 16 and 18 (NCGS 51-1, 51-2, 51-3, 15-6).

THE COMMON LAW MARRIAGE

A common law marriage is one that has not been solemnized by ceremony. The couple agree to live together as man and wife, and then publicly hold themselves out as being married. Common law marriages are not valid in North Carolina, but courts have ruled that if a couple move here from another state and that state recognized their common law marriage as being valid, then North Carolina will respect the laws of that state, and accept the couple as being married (*Parker v. Parker*, 265 S.E.2d 237 (NC 1980).

SAME SEX MARRIAGE

Vermont is the first state to recognize same sex marriages, which they refer to as a "civil union." Several other states, including North Carolina, have passed statutes, specifically denying marital status to couples of the same gender, regardless of whether that marriage is valid in another state (NCGS 51-1.2).

If you have any question about the validity of the decedent's marriage, then it is important to consult with an attorney.

THE LAWS OF DESCENT AND DISTRIBUTION

The North Carolina Laws of Descent and Distribution make a distinction between real and personal property. *Real property* is land and whatever is growing on or permanently attached to the land, such as a house. *Personal property* is everything else (money, securities, cars, paintings, etc.). If the decedent died without a Will, then his probate estate is distributed as follows:

✧ MARRIED, NO CHILD, NO PARENT
North Carolina law provides that if at the time of death the decedent was married and had no surviving *lineal descendant* (child, grandchild, great-grandchild, etc.), and no surviving parent, then all of his probate estate (real or personal) goes to his surviving spouse.

✧ MARRIED, NO CHILD, SURVIVING PARENT
If decedent was married and had no surviving lineal descendant, but he does have a surviving parent, then the spouse gets the first $50,000 and half of whatever personal property is left. The parent gets the other half. If both parents survive the decedent then they share that half equally. The spouse takes one half of the decedent's real property and surviving parent(s) inherit the other half.

✧ MARRIED, WITH CHILD OR DESCENDANTS OF THE CHILD
If the decedent was married and with one child, the spouse takes the first $30,000 and half of whatever personal property is left. The child takes the other half. The spouse inherits half of all real property and the child the other half. If the child dies before the decedent, leaving lineal descendants, then those lineal descendants inherit the child's share.

✧ MARRIED, WITH CHILDREN OR DESCENDANTS

If the decedent was married and with two or more children, the spouse takes the first $30,000 and one third of whatever personal property is left. The children share, equally, the remaining 2/3rds. The spouse inherits 1/3rd of the decedent's real property and the children share the remaining 2/3rds. If a child dies before the decedent, but leaves lineal descendants, then those lineal descendants inherit that child's share.

✧ SINGLE, WITH CHILDREN

If the decedent was not married when he died, but had children, then they share equally in the probate estate.

✧ SINGLE, NO CHILDREN

If the decedent had no surviving child or lineal descendants, then the property is divided equally between his parents. If only one of the decedent's parents is alive, then all of the property goes to that parent. If neither parent is alive, then the estate goes to the decedent's brothers and sisters. If a sibling died before the decedent, then that sibling's share goes to his children (the decedent's niece or nephew). If the deceased sibling had no surviving descendants, then the share is divided equally between the surviving siblings.

If the decedent had no brothers, sisters, nephews or nieces, then half of the estate goes to the decedent's grandparents on his mother's side and the other half goes to the decedent's grandparents on his father's side. If the maternal grandparents are deceased, then their share goes to their lineal descendants. If no lineal descendant survives them, then all of the estate goes to the paternal grandparents. Similarly, if the paternal grandparents are deceased, then their share goes to their lineal descendants, and if none their share goes to the maternal grandparents (NCGS 29-14, 29-15, 29-16).

THE AFTERBORN CHILD

If the decedent's relative was conceived before he died and born within 10 months after the date of death, then that child is entitled to receive as much of the decedent's intestate probate estate as if the child was alive at the time of his death (NCGS 29-9).

RELATIVES OF HALF-BLOOD

Relatives of half-blood inherit the same as if they were whole blood. For example, if the decedent had a brother from the same set of parents and a brother with the same father and a different mother, then both brothers inherit an equal share (NCGS 29-3).

✧ THE STATE: HEIR OF LAST RESORT

If a person dies without a Will and he has absolutely no relative who is entitled to inherit under North Carolina's Laws of Descent and Distribution, then the decedent's estate goes to the state of North Carolina (NCGS 29-12).

CAUTION   IT ISN'T ALL THAT SIMPLE

The explanation in this book of the North Carolina Laws of Descent and Distribution is abridged. Even though you may now know more about intestate succession than you ever wanted to know, there is much more to the law. For example, instead of taking the intestate share, the spouse can elect to take a one-third life estate interest in all of the real property owned by the decedent (NCGS 29-30).

Unless the distribution is straight forward such as all going to the spouse or to a child, it is best to consult with an attorney before deciding "who gets what."

WHO DIED FIRST?

Sometimes it happens that two family members die simultaneously, and no one knows who died first. For example, suppose a father and son die together in a car crash, how is the property distributed in that case?

Most Wills contain a provision saying that if the Will maker and any beneficiary die simultaneously, then the beneficiary is considered to have died first. For those who die without a Will, or if the Will is silent on the issue, North Carolina statute states that each person is assumed to have survived the other and the property of each is distributed on that basis.

In the above example, the father's property is distributed as if he survived his son and the son's property is distributed as if he survived his father. If the son had a $10,000 insurance policy with his father as beneficiary and his mother as alternate beneficiary, then the money will go to his mother.

If the father had a Will without any simultaneous death provision, then the Will is read as if the son died first. If the father left all of his property to his son and daughter, the daughter will inherit all of the father's property.

If the father and son owned property jointly, then if they die simultaneously, the property is divided with one half going to the estate of the father and the other half to the estate of his son (NCGS 28A-24-1, 28A-24-2, 28A-24-3, 28A-24-4).

THE RIGHTS OF A CHILD

ADOPTED CHILD

An adopted child has the same rights to inherit property from his adoptive parents as does a natural child. The adopted child does not have the right to inherit from his natural parents except if his parent was or is married to the adoptive parent. For example, if a child's mother marries and the child is later adopted by his stepfather, then the child still has full right to inherit from his mother. He also has the right to inherit from his adoptive father, but not from his natural father (NCGS 29-17).

NON-MARITAL CHILD

A child born out of wedlock has the same rights to inherit from his/her natural father as does one born in wedlock, provided:

☑ the decedent signed a declaration saying that the child is his and filed that declaration with the Clerk of the Superior Court in the county of his residence or that of the child's residence — or —

☑ The decedent's paternity was established by court

— or —

☑ The decedent signed a Will acknowledging the child as his own.

If the decedent denied his paternity, then it will take a court procedure to establish (or disprove) paternity. If you want to establish paternity, then you need to consult with an attorney who is experienced in litigation. You will need to notify the Personal Representative, in writing, that you are making a claim to inherit from the decedent's estate. This written notice must be given within 6 months of the date that the Personal Representative first publishes his notice to creditors of the decedent's estate (NCGS 29-19).

 **LAWYER**

NO SHARE FOR NEGLECTFUL PARENT

North Carolina statute does not allow a parent who has wilfully abandoned or neglected to support his minor child to inherit property from that minor child under the Laws of Descent and Distribution. The parent can inherit from a child under 18, if the abandoning parent resumed the maintenance and care of the child continuously for at least a year prior to the child's death.

The probate court is not going to deny a parent's inheritance unless evidence is presented that the parent abandoned the minor child. If you believe that a parent is not entitled to inherit the decedent's property on any of the above grounds, then you need to employ an attorney who is experienced in probate litigation to present such evidence to the court (NCGS 31A-2).

If a beneficiary has been convicted of causing the death of the decedent or being an accessory to the crime, then North Carolina law prohibits the killer from profiting from the crime. Property that the killer would have inherited either as a beneficiary of the Will or according to the Pennsylvania Laws of Descent and Distribution will be distributed as if the killer died before the decedent. For example, if the killer was the beneficiary of the decedent's life insurance policy, then the alternate beneficiary will get the insurance proceeds.

If the killer owned property with the decedent as a joint tenant with rights of survivorship (or as a Tenant by the Entirety), then the decedent share of that property will go to the decedent's estate and when the killer dies, the killer's share will also go to the decedent's estate (NCGS 31A-4, 31A-5, 31A-6).

 LAWYER

LAW SUIT FOR WRONGFUL DEATH

If anyone committed a wrongful act against the decedent that caused injury to the decedent or led to his death, then regardless of whether that person is convicted of the crime, the Personal Representative may sue that person for a wrongful death on behalf of the beneficiaries of the decedent's estate. There is a two year statute of limitations, so the suit needs to be brought within that time (NCGS 28A-18-2, 1-53).

WHEN TO CHALLENGE A WILL

It is not uncommon for a family member to be unhappy with the way the decedent willed his property. If you are tempted to challenge a Will, first consider whether the Will is valid under North Carolina law.

In North Carolina, a Will is presumed to be valid if at the time the decedent made the Will he was at least 18 years of age and of sound mind (NCGS 31-1).

The decedent acted with sound mind if:
- ☑ he knew what he was doing (namely making a Will);
- ☑ he knew what property he had;
- ☑ he remembered and understood his relationship to his family members and how they would be affected by his Will;
- ☑ he was not suffering from a delusional mental disorder affecting his ability to distribute his property.

The first step in the probate procedure is to have the Probate court determine whether the Will presented is valid. If the Will is in writing and signed by the Will maker in the presence of at least two credible witnesses, and a Notary Public, then there should be no problem in having the Will accepted into Probate.

If the Will was not notarized, but it was witnessed by two people (neither of whom have any interest in the Will), then such Will should be acceptable to the court. Before accepting the Will, the court will ask each witness to testify that he/she did see the Will signed in his/her presence.

THE UNWITNESSED WILL

It could happen that the decedent wrote out a Will in his own hand and signed it with no one present. Such a Will is called a **holographic Will.** Many states refuse to accept an unwitnessed Will into probate. The problem with a holographic Will is its authenticity. Because no one actually saw the decedent sign the Will, it is hard to determine whether the Will was written by the decedent or is a forgery. North Carolina courts have ruled that the Dead Man's Statute prohibits a witness, who has an interest in the case, from testifying that the decedent said he was writing out a Will or that he intended to leave a gift to someone (*In the Matter of Lamparter,* 497 S.E.2d 692, NC 1998).

Under North Carolina statute a holographic Will can be accepted into probate, provided:
⇨   The Will was signed by the decedent
                    and
⇨   The Will was written entirely in the decedent's hand
                    and
⇨   The Will was found after his death among his
      valuable papers or in his safe deposit box
(NCGS 31-3.4).

If the decedent left a holographic Will, then you need to consult with an attorney experienced in probate matters in order to present sufficient evidence to the court that the Will meets these requirements. The court will require three witnesses to testify that the Will was signed and written in the handwriting of the decedent. The court will also require testimony that the Will was found among the decedent's valuable papers, after his death (NCGS 31-18.2)

THE VERBAL WILL

Picture a death bed scene. The elderly gentleman is surrounded by several family members. In a whisper, just audible enough to be heard, he says:

"Even though I am a wealthy man, I never got around to making a Will. You all have been good to me, but I did want my entire fortune to go to my nephew, Robert. He has been like a son to me. "

Do you think Robert will inherit his uncle's estate?

If this took place in the state of North Carolina, then Robert might be in luck provided:
⇨ The uncle was about to die, and then he did, in fact, die.
⇨ There were two witnesses who will testify that the uncle specifically asked them to bear witness that this was his Will.

Of course, Robert would need to be extraordinarily lucky if that happened, considering that, in the absence of a Will, the family members would probably inherit the uncle's fortune under the Laws of Descent and Distribution.

And even if the Will were accepted into probate, North Carolina statute allows a verbal Will for personal property, only. If the uncle owned real property in the state of North Carolina, then his real property is inherited according to North Carolina's Laws of Descent and Distribution (NCGS 31-3.5).

READING THE WILL

If the decedent left a Will, then the Will states who is to receive the property. Most Wills are short and easy to read, however, you may come across an unfamiliar legal term such as the term *per stirpes*, for example:

"I leave the rest, residue and remainder of my
property to my children Darlena and Cassie,
in equal shares, per stirpes."

Because the children inherit the "... rest, residue and remainder.." they are the **residuary beneficiaries** of the probate estate and are entitled to whatever is left after the probate fees and costs, bills and taxes have been paid.

The term "per stirpes" means that if one of his daughters dies before he does (say Cassie) then the share intended for Cassie is to be divided equally among her descendants. Of course if Cassie leaves no descendants, then Darlena will inherit all of the property.

 **LAWYER**   THE AMBIGUOUS WILL

A Will is ambiguous if it is not clear or can be read two different ways. If you are having difficulty understanding what the decedent intended, then it is important to consult with an attorney. It may be necessary to have a court determine how the Will should be interpreted.

THE WILL THAT IS CONTRARY TO LAW

Sometimes a person who is of sound mind, makes a Will, but that Will has the effect of giving a spouse or a minor child less than is required under North Carolina law. One such example is that of Nancy. She didn't have an easy life. She worked long hours as a waitress. She divorced her hard drinking first husband. The final judgment gave her their homestead, some securities, and sole custody of their son. After the divorce Nancy had her attorney prepare a Will leaving all she owned to her son, Richard.

Some years later she met and married Harry, a chef at the restaurant where she worked. He moved into her home and they later had a daughter. Richard was 19, and his stepsister 12, when Nancy died after a lengthy battle with cancer.

Nancy was not a wealthy woman, but she did leave her car, her household furnishings, savings and securities worth $42,000, and the homestead. All of the property was in her name only.

Before she died, she told Richard, that she had not changed her Will because she wanted him to have all she owned. She said Harry had a good job and she was sure he would take good care of his daughter.

No sooner was the funeral over, when Nancy's son came in and demanded that Harry vacate his mother's home. Harry was furious and went to his attorney.

" Don't I have any rights? And how about my daughter? Doesn't she have any rights?"

The attorney was reassuring "Of course, you both do. Your daughter was born after your wife made her Will. If Nancy willed all of her property to you, then your daughter would not be entitled to anything. This is not the case here, so under North Carolina law she is entitled to receive as much as she would have if Nancy died without a Will (NCGS 31-5.5).

And you also have the right to inherit as much as you would have received if she died without a Will unless before Nancy died you:

☒ got a divorce; or

☒ voluntarily separated from your wife and lived in adultery without Nancy condoning such act; or

☒ wilfully and without just cause, abandoned and refused to live with Nancy, and was in fact not living with her when she died; or

☒ knowingly contracted a bigamous marriage.
(NCGS 31A-1)

"Of course not. I was a good husband to Nancy. I supported her and took care of her all during her illness. It was me, and not her son, who was at her side when she died."

The lawyer continued "And did you sign a prenuptial or postnuptial agreement giving up any rights you have as a spouse?"

"No, I signed nothing."

"In that case, you are entitled to 1/3rd of all of the real property owned by Nancy, with your child and stepchild sharing (equally) the other 2/3rds. You are also entitled to $30,000 plus 1/3rd of the remainder of your wife's personal property. The remaining 2/3rds goes to the children. You're lucky to have had a daughter with Nancy. The spouse of a second marriage is entitled to only half of his intestate share if the decedent had a child by a former marriage and none with the surviving spouse (NCGS 20-1)."

Harry wondered "How can my stepson get his 1/3rd of the house that me and my daughter are living in?"

"The house will need to be sold and the proceeds divided 3 ways."

Harry was concerned "But that means I need to move out of the house."

"Not necessarily, you could have the house appraised and purchase your stepson's share."

Harry said "Richard and I are not even talking to each other. What if Richard refuses to sell me his share?"

The lawyer answered "Then you are back to selling the house. There is another option, you could take a life estate interest in your wife's real property and keep all of the household furnishings instead of taking your intestate share. That means you keep the furnishings as your own and you have the right to live in the homestead until you die (NCGS 29-30)."

"But then I don't get the $30,000?"

The lawyer said "Yes but, you still can get $10,000 as a spousal allowance. Your daughter is entitled to $2,000 as a child's allowance. For that matter, Richard is also entitled to $2,000 because he is under 22 and a full time student."

"No, I think I'll take my spousal allowance and my intestate share. That's better than taking the life estate."

"Not so fast," the lawyer said "All of this is subject to court approval. Once the Will is filed with the court and a Personal Representative appointed, you can object to the Will by filing a dissent with the Clerk of the Superior Court. You have 6 months, but I suggest that you do so as soon as the Personal Representative is appointed (NCGS 30-1, 30-2, 30-3)."

The court did award a spousal and child allowance for each child. Harry received the $30,000 plus 1/3rd of the house. Richard did not fare as well. There was no cash left in the estate once the funeral expenses, medical bills, spousal allowance and the costs of probating the estate were paid. All that Richard received was his $2,000 allowance and his 1/3rd share of the house. And he didn't get that until the house was sold and his stepfather moved out a year later.

No doubt Nancy did not understand what would happen to her estate once she passed on. The Will she left did not accomplish her goal of providing for her son. All it did was cause turmoil and an irreparable rift between Harry and Richard. It didn't need to be that way. Had Nancy known about North Carolina law, she could have consulted with an attorney and set up an estate plan that could have provided for her son, without alienating her husband.

But, the moral of the story, for the purpose of this discussion, is that if you believe that the decedent's Will is not valid or is not drafted according to North Carolina law, then you need to consult with an attorney experienced in probate matters to determine your legal rights under that Will.

Getting Possession Of The Property

Knowing who is entitled to receive the decedent's property is one thing. Getting that property is another. As explained in the previous chapter if the property is held jointly with someone, or in a trust for someone, then the property belongs to the joint owner or beneficiary and that person can get possession of the property simply by giving a certified copy of the death certificate to the financial institution.

If the decedent held property in his name only, then some sort of probate procedure is necessary in order to transfer ownership to the proper beneficiary. In North Carolina, most probate procedures require the assistance of an attorney, but there are a few items that you can obtain on your own.

This chapter explains the various probate procedures and when it is appropriate to use that procedure.

DISTRIBUTING PERSONAL PROPERTY

Too often, the first person to discover the body will help himself to the decedent's *personal effects* (clothing, jewelry, appliances, electrical equipment, cameras, books, household items and furnishing, etc.). Unless that person is the decedent's sole beneficiary, such action is unconscionable, if not illegal.

If the decedent left a Will, then the personal property goes to the beneficiaries named in the Will. If the decedent did not leave a Will, then the North Carolina Rules of Descent and Distribution determine who is to inherit his personal effects (see page 110).

All of the personal effects should be turned over to the Personal Representative. The Personal Representative then has the duty to distribute the property according to the decedent's Will, or if no Will, then according to the North Carolina Rules of Descent and Distribution.

If you determine that there is no need for a Probate procedure and the decedent did not have a Will then his next of kin need to divide all of the personal effects among themselves according to the North Carolina Rules of Descent and Distribution. Most personal effects have little, if any, monetary value. Furniture may be worth less than it costs to ship. In such case, the beneficiaries may decide to donate the personal property to the decedent's favorite charity.

WHAT'S EQUAL?

The decedent's Will or if no Will, then the North Carolina Laws of Descent and Distribution may direct that the decedent's personal property be divided equally between two or more beneficiaries. The problem with the term "equal" is that people have different ideas of what "equal" means. Unless there is clear evidence that the decedent's Will meant something else, "equal" refers to the monetary value of the item and not to the number of items received. For example, to divide the decedent's personal effects equally, one beneficiary may receive an expensive item of jewelry and another beneficiary may receive several items whose overall value is approximately equal to that single piece of jewelry.

When distributing personal effects there needs to be cooperation and perhaps compromise, or else bitter arguments might arise over items of little monetary value.

One such argument occurred when an elderly woman died who was rich only in her love for her five children and 12 grandchildren. After the funeral, the children gathered in their mother's apartment. Each child had his/her own furnishings and no need for anything in the apartment. They agreed to donate all of their mother's personal effects to a local charity with the exception of a few items of sentimental value.

Each child took some small item as a remembrance —
a handkerchief, a large platter that their mother used to
serve family dinners, a doily their mother crocheted.
Things went smoothly until it came to her photograph
album. Frank, the youngest sibling, said, "I'll take this."
Marie objected saying, "But there are pictures in that
album that I want."

Frank retorted, "You already took all the pictures Mom
had on her dresser."

The argument went downhill from there. Unsettled
sibling rivalries boiled over, fueled by the hurt of the loss
that they were all experiencing.

It almost came to blows when the eldest settled the
argument: "Frank you make copies of all of the photos in
the album for Marie. Marie, you make copies of all of the
pictures that you took and give them to Frank. This way
you both will have a complete set of Mom's pictures.

And while you're at it, make copies for the rest of us."

THE SMALL ESTATE AFFIDAVIT

Suppose the only item that the decedent had in his name only was a bank account worth $4,000. If the net value of all of the decedent's personal property is not greater than $10,000, then the proper beneficiary can get possession of that account without going through a full probate procedure. To get the money the beneficiary can give the bank a SMALL ESTATE AFFIDAVIT. An *Affidavit* is a written statement of facts made by someone (the "Affiant") that is signed in the presence of a Notary Public. To use the Small Estate Affidavit, the Affiant must swear or acknowledge to the Notary Public that following facts are true:

- ☑ The net value** of the decedent's personal property is not greater than $10,000.
- ☑ If the spouse is the sole heir, then the net value** is not greater than $20,000.
- ☑ No probate procedure is pending.
- ☑ Thirty days have passed since the death.

** The *net value* is the current market value of the property less monies owed on the property.

You may be thinking "This is easy. All I need to do is sign an Affidavit and I can get any of the decedent's personal property up to $10,000 (or $20,000 for a spouse)." But it isn't quite that simple. You need to take possession of the property, responsibly. If the decedent owed money, then you need to use the funds to pay the bills. If there is an allowance due to the spouse or child, then that needs to be paid. And you need to file the Small Estate Affidavit with the Clerk of the Superior Court. Finally, within 90 days, you need to file a Final Affidavit showing that debts were paid and monies distributed to the proper beneficiary (NCGS 28A-25-1, 28A-25-1.1, 28A-25-3).

If it later turns out that a full probate procedure is necessary, then you or whoever took possession of the personal property will need to deliver that property to the Personal Representative. If monies were used to pay bills, then the Affiant will need to account to the Personal Representative (NCGS 28A-25-5).

The Small Estate Affidavit is not the way to go if the decedent owned real property as a Tenant in Common or in his name only. In such case, a full probate procedure is necessary, and any personal property can be distributed as part of that probate procedure.

A Small Estate Affidavit is the way to go if the value of the personal property to be transferred is under $10,000 (or $20,000 if spouse is sole heir) and:

☑ no probate procedure is necessary, and

☑ there is only one heir, or if more than one, they all agree to the distribution, and

☑ provision has been made to pay any outstanding bill.

There is a sample Affidavit on the opposite page. This Affidavit can be used if the decedent died without a Will. See the next page for an Affidavit that can be used if the decedent had a Will.

SMALL ESTATE AFFIDAVIT
pursuant to NCGS 28A-25-1 (intestate)

STATE OF NORTH CAROLINA, COUNTY OF _____

The Affiant _____, first being duly sworn deposes and says:

1. My name and address is:

Name _____

Address _____

_____

2. The decedent's name is _____.
and his residence at time of death is _____

_____

3. The date and place of death of the decedent:

Date _____ Place _____

4. The decedent died intestate. My relationship to the decedent is _____ and I am the decedent's heir. Thirty days have elapsed since the date of death of the decedent.

5. The value of all the personal property owned by the estate of the decedent, less liens and encumbrances thereon, does not exceed $10,000. If the spouse is the sole heir, then the personal property does not exceed $20,000.

6. No application or petition for appointment of a personal representative is pending or has been granted in any jurisdiction.

7. The names and addresses of those persons who are entitled, under the provisions of the Intestate Succession Act, to the personal property of the decedent and their relationship, if any, to the decedent are as follows

NAME   RELATIONSHIP   ADDRESS

_____

_____

8. A description sufficient to identify each tract of real property owned by the decedent at the time of his death is:

_____

_____

Sworn to and subscribed before me on this day _____

_____
NOTARY PUBLIC

SMALL ESTATE AFFIDAVIT
pursuant to NCGS 28A-25-2 (testate)

STATE OF NORTH CAROLINA, COUNTY OF _____
The Affiant _____, first being duly sworn deposes and says:

1. My name and address is:
Name   _____
Address _____
_____

2. The decedent's name is _____.
and his residence at time of death is _____
_____

3. The date and place of death of the decedent:
Date _____ Place _____

4. My relationship to the decedent is _____ and I am the decedent's heir. Thirty days have elapsed since the date of death of the decedent.

5. The decedent died testate. A certified copy of the decedent's will is attached to this affidavit. The will has been admitted to probate in the court of the proper county and a duly certified copy of the will has been recorded in each county in which is located any real property owned by the decedent at the time of his death.

6. The value of all the personal property owned by the estate of the decedent, less liens and encumbrances thereon, does not exceed $10,000. If the spouse is the sole heir, then the personal property does not exceed $20,000.

7. No application or petition for appointment of a personal representative is pending or has been granted in any jurisdiction.

8. The names and addresses of those persons who are entitled, under the provisions of the will to the personal property of the decedent and their relationship, if any, to the   decedent are as follows

NAME   RELATIONSHIP   ADDRESS

_____

_____

9. A description sufficient to identify each tract of real property owned by the decedent at the time of his death is:

_____

_____

Sworn to and subscribed before me on this day _____

_____
NOTARY PUBLIC

COMPLETING THE AFFIDAVIT

Notice that you need to attach a certified copy of the Will to the Affidavit. You can get that certified copy from the Clerk of the Superior Court in the county where the decedent lived. You may save time if you first call the Clerk. Some questions you might want answered are:

How do I get to the Court house?

What is the best time to meet with you?

What documents do I need to bring with me?

How much will it cost to file?

Is a personal check acceptable or do I need to bring cash or a money order?

COMPLETING THE SMALL ESTATE PROCEDURE

Once you have properly filed the Small Estate Affidavit with the Clerk of the Superior Court, the Clerk will record the document and then mail a copy to the persons shown in the Affidavit as being entitled to the property.

Once you receive the copy of the Affidavit from the Clerk of the Superior Court, you can take it to whomever has the decedent's property, and they will turn over the property to you. You should have no problem collecting the personal property because North Carolina statue 28A-25-2 states that if anyone refuses to honor that Affidavit, then you can sue them and they will need to give you the item and pay your attorney's fees and costs.

As explained once the decedent's bills are paid and the property distributed to the proper beneficiary, then you need to file the final Affidavit with the Clerk. The Clerk should have the final Affidavit form for you to complete. The Affidavit will state what property was collected and how those funds were used to pay estate debts (the court filing fees, funeral expenses, etc.) with the remainder given to the proper beneficiary.

INCOME TAX REFUNDS

You need to file the decedent's final income tax return (IRS form 1040) by April 15th of the year following the year in which he died. If there is a refund due to the decedent and you are entitled to that money as the beneficiary of the decedent, then you can obtain the refund by filing IRS form 1310 along with the 1040. You can obtain form 1310 from the decedent's accountant, or if he did not have an accountant and you wish to file yourself, then call the IRS at (800) 829-3676 to obtain the proper form. You can obtain instructions, publications and form from the Internal Revenue Service Web site:

 IRS WEB SITE
IRS FORMS AND INSTRUCTIONS
http://www.irs.ustreas.gov/prod/forms_pubs/forms.html
IRS PUBLICATIONS
http://www.irs.ustreas.gov/prod/forms_pubs/pubs.html

If you are appointed as Personal Representative, you do not need to file form 1310 because once you file the decedent's final income tax return, any refund will be forwarded to you as Personal Representative. Similarly, a surviving spouse does not need to file form 1310 because the spouse will automatically receive any refund due on their joint income tax return.

North Carolina statute provides that any federal tax refund up to $500, shall be given to the spouse and shall become the sole and separate property of the spouse. If the decedent filed a separate return, then any refund up to $250 goes to the surviving spouse. Anything in excess of these amounts shall be divided with half going to the spouse and half to the decedent's estate (NCGS 28A-15-6, 28A-15-9).

THE STATE INCOME TAX REFUND

The decedent's final North Carolina State income tax return needs to be filed at the same time the federal income tax return is filed. If the Personal Representative files the return, then any refund will be given to him to be deposited to the estate account. If no probate procedure is necessary, then the next of kin can file the return. If you need information about filing the final return, you can call (919) 733-4682 or you can visit the Department of Revenue Web site:

 NC DEPARTMENT OF REVENUE WEB SITE
http://www.DOR.STATE.NC.US/DOR/

If there is a refund due, and that sum does not exceed $200, the Department of Revenue will give the check to the surviving spouse. If the decedent was single, or if the refund is greater than $200, the Department of Revenue will forward the check to the Clerk of the Superior Court in the county of the decedent's residence. The next of kin can get possession of the funds by contacting the Clerk (NCGS 28A-15-8).

DEPOSITING THE TAX REFUND

If the refund check is sent to the Personal Representative, then he will deposit it the to estate account. If there is no probate procedure and the refund check (or any other check made out to the decedent) is in the name of the decedent, you can deposit the check to the decedent's bank account. You can obtain all of the money in that account by using whatever probate procedure is appropriate depending on the value of the estate. If the decedent does not have a bank account, and the refund is less than $5,000, you can deposit the check with the Clerk of the Superior Court and the Clerk will give the funds to the appropriate heir (NCGS 28A-25-6)

TRANSFERRING THE CAR

If the decedent owned a motor vehicle, then title to the car needs to be transferred to the new owner and new owner needs to register the car in the state where it will be driven. You may want to limit the use of the car until it is transferred to the beneficiary. If the decedent's car is involved in an accident before the car is transferred to the new owner, then the decedent's estate may be liable for the damage. Having adequate insurance on the car may save the estate from monetary loss, but a pending lawsuit could delay the probate procedure and prevent any money from being distributed to the beneficiaries until the lawsuit is settled.

We have discussed how title is transferred if the car was held jointly (see page 100). If the car was in the decedent's name only, and there is a probate procedure then it is the Personal Representative's job to transfer the motor vehicles to the proper beneficiary. If the decedent had a Will and he made a specific gift of the car to someone, then the Personal Representative will transfer the car to that person. If there was no mention of the car in his Will, then the car goes to the residuary beneficiaries under the Will.

If the decedent was survived by a spouse, then the spouse can take the car as part of the spouse's allowance. If the decedent did not have a Will, then the car goes to the decedent's heirs as determined by the North Carolina Laws of Descent and Distribution (see page 110).

⬤ MAKING THE TRANSFER 🚐

If no probate procedure is necessary, you can transfer the car using the Small Estate Affidavit provided the car is worth $10,000 or less ($20,000 if transferred to the spouse). Once you have the Affidavit, the Department of Motor Vehicles will help you through the process of transferring title to the motor vehicle. See page 100 for their telephone number and Web site.

TRANSFER WHEN MORE THAN ONE BENEFICIARY
If there is more than one person who has the right to inherit the car, then they all can take title to the car. That may not be a practical thing to do since only one person can drive the car at any given time and if one gets into an accident, then they all can be held liable. The better route is for the beneficiaries to agree to have one person take title to the car. The person taking title will need to compensate the others for their share of the car. In such case the beneficiaries need to come to an agreement as to the value of the car.

DETERMINING THE VALUE OF THE CAR
Cars are valued in many different ways. The *collateral* value of the car is the value that banks use to evaluate the car for purposes of making a loan to the owner of the car. Because banks print these values in book form, the collateral value is also referred to as the *book value* of the car. If you were to trade in a car for the purpose of purchasing a new car, then the car dealer will offer you the *wholesale* value of the car. Were you to purchase that same car from a car dealer, then he will price it at its *retail* or *fair market value*. Usually the retail price is highest, wholesale is lowest and the book value of the car is somewhere in between.

You can call your local bank to get the book value of the car. It may be more difficult to obtain the wholesale value of the car because the amount of money a dealer is willing to pay for the car depends on the value of the new car that you are purchasing. You can determine the car's retail value by looking at comparable used car advertisements in the local newspaper or over the Internet.

TRANSFERRING THE MOBILE HOME

A mobile home is a motor vehicle, so the methods described can be used to transfer the decedent's mobile home. Before transferring the motor vehicle, you need to find out whether the land on which the mobile home is located was leased or owned by the decedent.

If the decedent was renting space in a trailer park, then you need to contact the trailer park owner to transfer the lease agreement to the beneficiary of the mobile home. If the decedent owned the land under the mobile home, then a probate procedure will be necessary to transfer the land to the proper beneficiary. See page 141 for information about transferring real property.

The leased car is not an asset of the estate because the decedent did not own the car. The leased car is a liability to the estate because the decedent was obligated to pay the balance of the monies owed on the lease agreement. The Personal Representative, or next of kin, needs to work out an agreement with the company to either assign the lease to a beneficiary or family member who will agree to pay for the lease — or to have the estate pay off the lease by purchasing the car under the terms of the lease agreement.

Some lenders will allow the lease to be assigned to a beneficiary provided the estate remains liable for the balance of payment. In such cases, it is better to have the beneficiary refinance the car and have the original lease agreement paid in full.

If the remaining payments exceed the current market value of the car, there may be a temptation to hand the keys over to the leasing company. This may not be the best strategy, because the leasing company can then sell the car and then sue the estate for the balance of the monies owed. If the decedent had no assets or if the only assets he had are creditor proof, then simply returning the car may be an option. But if the decedent's estate has assets available to pay the balance of the lease payments, then the Personal Representative needs to arrange to have the car transferred in a way that releases the estate from all further liability.

TRANSFERRING REAL PROPERTY

If the decedent owned real property in his name only, or if the decedent owned property as a Tenant in Common, then a full probate procedure will be necessary in order to transfer the parcel to the proper beneficiary. No probate procedure is necessary to transfer North Carolina real property if the decedent held that property:

⇨   as the owner of a life estate   — or —

⇨   jointly *with right of survivorship*   — or —

⇨   as tenants by the entirety (i.e., as husband and wife)

As explained in Chapter 5, upon the decedent's death the survivors have full ownership of the property. All that need be done is to record the death certificate. In North Carolina, the Register of Deeds in the county of the decedent's residence will record that death certificate. If the property is located in any other county, then you need to make arrangements to have the death certificate recorded in that county.

Call the Register of Deeds in that county and ask where to mail the death certificate and how much money you need to send for the recording fee. Enclose a self addressed stamped envelop for the clerk to return the recorded death certificate to you so you will have a record of where the certificate is recorded.

Once the death certificate is recorded any one who examines the county record will know of the death of the decedent and that the surviving owners now have full authority to occupy or transfer the property.

SUMMARY ADMINISTRATION

A full probate procedure is designed to protect creditors of the decedent's estate as well as the beneficiaries of the estate. The creditors are protected because the court will see to it that they are notified of the death and given an opportunity to come forward and make a claim for monies owed to them. The beneficiaries are protected because the court sees to it that they are given a full accounting of what is in the Probate Estate, how the estate monies are spent during the probate procedure and then finally, that each heir receives his/her proper share of the estate. All these safeguards take time and money. Sometimes it is pointless to go through all this "red tape" because there is only one beneficiary, and the decedent didn't owe any money.

A *Summary Administration* is a short, expedited probate procedure designed to distribute the decedent's estate quickly in such cases. Each state has different criteria as to when it is appropriate to use a Summary Administration. In North Carolina, the procedure is available to a surviving spouse, provided all the following are true:

⇨ the spouse is the sole heir

⇨ if the decedent had a Will, the Will does not prohibit Summary Administration, and any executor named in the Will has been notified of the spouse's request for Summary Administration

⇨ no one has asked the court to be appointed as Personal Representative

⇨ the spouse agrees to be personally liable for all claims against the estate (including taxes) up to the value of the Probate Estate.

To get a Summary Administration, the spouse will need to file a *petition* (a request to the court) with the Clerk of the Superior Court. If the Clerk determines that the petition and the accompanying evidence comply with the statute, then the Clerk will issue an order of Summary Administration and the spouse can use the order to get possession of the property (NCGS 28A-28-1, 28A-28-2, 28A-28-3, 28A-28-4).

But how do you do it?

Although the statute says the spouse is entitled to Summary Administration, it does not tell you how to do it. Clerks in the Superior Court are most courteous but it is not in their job description to provide legal advice to you. If you want to do a Summary Administration, then you have three options:

➤ go to a law library and research the subject

➤ purchase a book or computer kit that gives you the forms and explains how to go through the process.

➤ consult with a probate attorney.

You may find that, in the long run, the third option will cost you less in time and money.

THE FULL PROBATE PROCEDURE

If the decedent left real property in his name only or if the decedent left assets worth more than $10,000 that goes to someone other than the spouse, then there needs to be a full Probate Administration. The procedure can take anywhere from several months to more than a year depending on the size and complexity of the Probate Estate. It is the Personal Representative's job to use the Probate Estate to pay all valid claims and then to distribute what is left to the proper beneficiary.

All of the decedent's debts are paid from the Probate Estate and not from Personal Representative's pocket; but if the Personal Representative makes a mistake then he may be responsible to pay for that mistake. For example, if the Personal Representative pays a debt that did not need to be paid — or if the Personal Representative transfers property to the beneficiaries too quickly and there were still taxes due on the estate, then he may be responsible to pay for such error (NCGS 28A-13-10).

The Personal Representative needs to employ an attorney to guide him through the process. It then becomes the job of the attorney for the Personal Representative to see to it that the estate is administered properly and without any personal liability to the Representative. The attorney has the right to receive reasonable fees for his services and those fees are a proper charge to the decedent's Estate. The attorney can charge a flat fee as a percentage of the estate or he can charge on an hourly basis. Hourly fees can run anywhere from $175 an hour to $300 an hour depending on the complexity of the case.

The first step in the Probate procedure is to have someone appointed by the court as the Personal Representative. If there is a Will, the court will appoint the person named as Executor of the Will. If the named Executor cannot or refuses to serve or if the decedent died intestate, then anyone with priority can file a petition (request) to be appointed. North Carolina statute 28A-4-1 gives an order of priority for appointing a Personal Representative:

1. The surviving spouse
2. Anyone entitled to take property under the provisions of the decedent's Will
3. Anyone entitled to inherit property under the North Carolina Laws of Descent and Distribution.
4. Any next of kin
5. Any of the decedent's creditors
6. Anyone of good character who lives in the county
7. Anyone of good character who is qualified to serve under North Carolina statute.

If two people of the same priority apply, then the Clerk of the Superior will decide who shall serve. If you have an objection to the appointment of someone who has priority, then you can raise those concerns to the Clerk.

YOUR RIGHTS AS A BENEFICIARY

If you are the beneficiary of an estate, then you have many rights.

✧   RIGHT TO YOUR OWN ATTORNEY

The attorney who handles the estate is employed by and represents the Personal Representative. If the estate is sizeable, then you might consider employing your own attorney to check that things are done properly and in a timely manner. If you are not in a financial position to employ an attorney, then you can do the following things to protect you interests:

✧   RIGHT TO A COPY OF THE WILL

If there is a Will then you have the right to receive a copy of that Will. Once the Personal Representative is appointed have him or his attorney forward the copy to you.

✧   RIGHT TO DEMAND SUFFICIENT BOND

It doesn't happen often, but every now and again a Personal Representative will run off with estate funds. A bond is insurance for the estate. If estate monies are stolen then the company that issued the bond will reimburse the estate for the loss. No bond is required by law unless the Will requires that the Personal Representative be bonded or unless the Personal Representative lives out of state. If you have concern about the safety of the estate funds, you can ask the court to require bond. Before making the request, consider that the cost of the bond is paid by the estate. If real property cannot be transferred without a court order, then it may be sufficient just to cover the value of the personal property (NCGS 28A-8-1, 28A-8-3).

✧ RIGHT TO COPY OF INVENTORY

The Personal Representative must file an inventory of all of the assets of the Probate Estate within 3 months of his appointment. You can ask him or his attorney to give you a copy of the inventory as soon as it is filed with the court (NCGS 28A-20-1).

✧ RIGHT TO COPIES OF TAX RETURNS

It is important that you receive copies of all tax returns that the Personal Representative is obliged to file. If the Personal Representative fails to file a return, or fails to pay taxes, or if he under-reports a tax obligation, then you could later be called on to pay estate taxes out of the proceeds that you receive.

✧ RIGHT TO AN ACCOUNTING

The Personal Representative must file an accounting within one year of his appointment or within six months after receiving a tax release from the state of North Carolina. You should receive a copy of the accounting as soon as the Personal Representative files it with the court.

The accounting should start with the inventory value of the estate and end with the amount of money that will be left to distribute after all the bills have been paid. If the estate has significant assets you may want your own accountant or attorney look over the final accounting to be sure it is correct (NCGS 28A-21-2).

✧   RIGHT TO APPROVE FEES

The Personal Representative is entitled to receive a *commission* (compensation) for his work in administering the estate. The amount must be approved by the Clerk of the Superior Court. The maximum amount that can be awarded is 5% of the value of the personal property which are probate assets plus 5% of the receipts and expenditures which are fairly made during the course of the administration. The value of the expenditures includes the value of the spousal or child's allowance that may be set aside from the claims of creditors (see Page 88) (NCGS 28A-23-3).

If the Personal Representative is also a beneficiary of the estate he may decide not to take a commission and just take his inheritance. The reason may be economic. Any fee he takes is taxable as ordinary income, but monies inherited are not taxable to him as a beneficiary. Ask the Personal Representative to tell you, in writing, whether he intends to ask as a fee, and if so, how much.

The attorney for the Personal Representative is also entitled to reasonable compensation. Ask the Personal Representative to give you a copy of the retainer agreement that he signed with his attorney, so that you will know how much is being charged for legal fees. If the attorney is employed on an hourly basis, have the attorney give a written estimate of the time he expects to expend on the probate procedure.

If you think either of these fees are unreasonable, then you have the right to negotiate to reduce the amount. If you cannot come to an agreement, then consider consulting with your own attorney to present your concerns to the court.

IT'S YOUR RIGHT - DON'T BE INTIMIDATED

You may feel uncomfortable being assertive with a friend or family member who is Personal Representative. Don't be. It's your money and your legal right to be kept informed. Be especially firm if the Decedent's Representative waives you off with:

"You've known me for years. Surely you trust me."

People who are trustworthy, don't ask to be trusted. They do what is right. The very fact that the Personal Representative is resisting, is a red flag. In such case, you can explain that it is not a matter of trust, but a matter of what is your legal right.

At the same time, keep things in perspective. Your family relationship may be more important, than the money you inherit. The job of Personal Representative is often complex and demanding. If the Personal Representative is getting the job done, then let him know that you appreciate his efforts.

THE CHECK LIST

We have discussed many things that need to be done when someone dies in the state of North Carolina. The next page contains a check list that you may find helpful.

You can check those items that you need to do, and then cross them off the list once they are done. We made the list as comprehensive as possible, so many items may not apply in your case. In such case, you can cross them off the list or mark them *N/A* (not applicable).

Things to do

FUNERAL ARRANGEMENTS TO BE MADE
☐ AUTOPSY ☐ ANATOMICAL GIFT
☐ DISPOSITION OF BODY OR ASHES

DEATH CERTIFICATE
GIVE COPY TO: _____

_____

_____

NOTICE OF DEATH
PEOPLE TO BE NOTIFIED _____

COMPANIES TO NOTIFY
☐ TELEPHONE COMPANY
    ☐ LOCAL CARRIER ☐ LONG DISTANCE ☐ CELLULAR
☐ NEWSPAPER (OBITUARY PRINTED)
☐ NEWSPAPER CANCELLED   ☐ deposit refund
☐ SOCIAL SECURITY
☐ INTERNET SERVER
☐ TELEVISION CABLE COMPANY
☐ POWER & LIGHT   ☐ deposit refund
☐ POST OFFICE
☐ OTHER UTILITIES (GAS, WATER)   ☐ deposit refund
☐ PENSION PLAN
☐ ANNUITY
☐ HEALTH INSURANCE COMPANY
☐ LIFE INSURANCE COMPANY
☐ HOME INSURANCE COMPANY
☐ MOTOR VEHICLE INSURANCE COMPANY
☐ CONDOMINIUM OR HOMEOWNER ASSOCIATION
☐ CANCEL SERVICE CONTRACT   ☐ deposit refund
☐ CREDIT CARD COMPANIES _____

_____

_____

Things to do

REMOVE DECEDENT AS BENEFICIARY OF:
- ☐ WILL   ☐ INSURANCE POLICY   ☐ PENSION PLAN
- ☐ BANK OR IRA ACCOUNT   ☐ SECURITY

DEBTS
PAY DECEDENT'S DEBTS (AMOUNT & CREDITOR)

_____

COLLECT MONIES OWED TO DECEDENT (AMOUNT & DEBTOR)

_____

TAXES
- ☐ FILE FINAL FEDERAL INCOME TAX RETURN
- ☐ FILE FINAL STATE INCOME TAX RETURN
- ☐ RECEIVE INCOME TAX REFUND
- ☐ FILE ESTATE TAX RETURN

PROPERTY TO BE TRANSFERRED
- ☐ PERSONAL EFFECTS
- ☐ MOTOR VEHICLE
- ☐ BANK ACCOUNT
- ☐ CREDIT UNION ACCOUNT
- ☐ IRA ACCOUNT
- ☐ SECURITIES
- ☐ BROKERAGE ACCOUNT
- ☐ INSURANCE PROCEEDS
- ☐ HOMESTEAD
- ☐ TIME SHARE
- ☐ OTHER REAL PROPERTY
- ☐ CONTENTS OF SAFE DEPOSIT BOX

OTHER THINGS TO DO

_____
_____
_____

Preneed Arrangements 7

Death is a wake-up call because once someone close to us dies we are reminded of our own mortality. Many believe that death can be put off, but the inevitable is inevitable. Although we cannot change the fact of our death, we have the power to control the circumstances of our death by making preneed arrangements.

You can make preneed arrangements so that you will be buried in the manner you wish and where you wish. You can also make arrangements that direct the kind of medical treatments you want to be given in the event you become seriously ill.

You can legally appoint someone to make your medical decisions in the event that you are too ill to speak for yourself. If you let that person know how you feel about life support systems, autopsies and anatomical gifts then that person will be authorized to act on your behalf and will see to it that your wishes are carried out.

As this chapter will show, it is relatively simple and inexpensive to make such preneed arrangements.

MAKING BURIAL ARRANGEMENTS

When making burial arrangements for the decedent, you may decide to purchase one or more burial spaces nearby for yourself or other family members.

If the decedent was buried in the family plot, then this is the time to take inventory of the number of spaces left and who in the family expects to use those spaces.

If all of the spaces are taken and if you plan to be cremated, then as explained in Chapter 1, some cemeteries will allow an urn to be placed in an occupied family plot. You can call the cemetery and ask them to explain their policy as it relates to the burial of an urn in a currently occupied grave site or mausoleum.

If this is not an option, and the cemetery of your choice has a columbarium, you might consider purchasing a space at this time.

If you wish to have your cremains scattered, then you need to let your next of kin know where and how this is to be done.

VETERAN OR
VETERAN'S SPOUSE

If you are an honorably discharged veteran, you have the right to be buried in a Veterans National Cemetery. You cannot reserve a grave site in advance. If your Veteran spouse was buried in a Veterans National Cemetery then you have the right to be buried in that same grave site unless soil conditions require a separate grave site.

If you wish to be buried in a Veterans National Cemetery, then check on current availability (see page 14 for telephone numbers). Let your next of kin know your choice of cemetery.

To establish your eligibility your next of kin will need to provide the following information:

➤ the veteran's rank, serial, social security and VA claim numbers

➤ the branch of service; the date and place of entry into and separation from the service

The next of kin will also need to provide the VA with a copy of the veteran's official military discharge document bearing an official seal or a DD 214 form.

If you wish to be buried in a national cemetery, then you need to make all of these items readily accessible to your family.

If you are financially able, in addition to purchasing a burial space, consider purchasing a Preneed funeral plan. It will be easier on your family emotionally and financially if you make your own funeral arrangements. If you do not have sufficient cash on hand for the kind of funeral you desire, then many funeral directors offer an installment payment plan.

Once you decide on a plan, the funeral director will present you with a contract. The print may be small, but it is worth your effort to read it before signing. If the contract is written in "legalese" then either consult with your attorney before signing it or ask as many questions of the funeral director as is necessary to make the terms of the contract clear to you.

If you are not satisfied with the way a certain section of the contract is written then add an addendum to the contract that explains, in plain English, your understanding of that passage. If you are concerned about something that is not mentioned in the contract, then insist that the contract be amended to include that item.

In particular, check to see whether the contract answers the following questions.

How are your contract funds protected?

North Carolina laws are designed to protect the purchaser of a Preneed funeral plan. According to North Carolina law, you have the option of having the funds you give to the funeral firm placed in a trust account, or you can purchase a Prearrangement Insurance Policy. The Prearrangement policy can be a life insurance policy or an annuity that will fund the Preneed Funeral Contract at the time of your death.

Check to see if your Preneed contract states how your monies will be protected. If the funds are protected by being placed in a trust account, then under North Carolina law, the funeral firm is allowed to keep 10% of the monies paid. The remaining 90% must be placed into the trust account. Have the funeral firm agree to furnish you with proof of the deposit once the contract is signed. Have the funeral firm promise, in writing, to notify you should they decide to change banks (NCGS 90-210.61).

If you are purchasing a Prearrangement Insurance Policy, then North Carolina law requires that you be given the name of the insurance company and their relationship to the funeral firm. If you are paying the policy on an installment basis, then the contract needs to disclose the penalty should you fail to make payment. And you also need to know how much you will forfeit should you cancel after you have made full payment of the purchase price (NCGS 58-60-35).

Does the contract cover all costs?

The contract should contain an itemized list stating exactly what goods and services are included in the sales price. Ask the funeral director whether there will be any additional cost when you die. For example, if you have not purchased a burial space, then that cost needs to be factored in. If you made provision for a burial space, then you need to make the funeral director aware of where you have arranged to be buried. If you have not made such provision, then the funeral director can assist you in making burial arrangements.

Is the price guaranteed?

You can purchase a Standard Preneed Funeral Contract or an inflation-proof contract. If you purchase the Standard plan, then the price for the goods and services that you have chosen under those contracts is not fixed, and the company can charge additional monies upon your death. The Inflation-proof contract guarantees that the goods and services you choose will be provided upon your death, regardless of when you finally die. If you choose the Inflation-proof contract, then once the contract is performed, the funeral firm has the right to keep all of the Trust funds on deposit (or all of the insurance proceeds) even if those funds are in excess of the cost of the goods and services actually provided. Your contract should disclose this information to you (NCGS 90-210.62).

Can you cancel the contract?

If you purchased the Preneed contract in your home, then you have a three day "cooling off" period. This means that you can cancel the contract and receive all of your money back provided you cancel the contract no later than midnight of the third business day after you signed the Agreement (NCGS 25A-39).

If you purchased the contract somewhere other than your home, then your contract should say whether and under what terms you can cancel the contract.

FOR REVOCABLE CONTRACTS

If your funds are being held in a trust account, then once you cancel the contract, the bank must return all of the trust funds to you within 30 days of your written request for the funds. The funeral firm places only 90% of the monies you paid in the trust account. Your contract will probably state that should you cancel the contract, the firm keeps the 10%.

If you purchased a Prearrangement Insurance Policy, then within 30 days of your written notice to cancel, they must return the amount as stated in your contract. You need to check to see what percentage of monies that you paid will be forfeited in the event that you revoke the agreement (NCGS 90-210.65).

FOR IRREVOCABLE CONTRACTS

If you purchase an *irrevocable* contract (one that can't be cancelled), then North Carolina statute gives your Personal Representative the right to substitute a different funeral firm to furnish the goods and services. This protects you in the event that you die in another state or country (NCGS 90-210.63).

Revocable or irrevocable, it is a good idea to have the contract spell out what provision will be made in the event that you move to another state or in the event you happen to die in another state or country. Many funeral firms are part of a national funeral service corporation with funeral firms located throughout the United States, so this is not usually a problem.

CHANGING TO AN IRREVOCABLE CONTRACT

People who apply for Medicaid, Supplemental Security Income ("SSI") or other public assistance program cannot qualify for these programs if their assets exceed a given amount (usually $2,000). A revocable contract is considered to be an asset because the person can cash it in. If the contract is irrevocable, then it does not count as an asset and does not affect a person's ability to qualify for the program. If you purchase a revocable contract and then later need to apply for any of these programs you may need to have the contract changed to one that is irrevocable. Check to see that your contract allows you to make such a change without any penalty to you.

Is the funeral firm reputable?

The state of North Carolina has established a Preneed Recovery Funds to reimburse buyers of a Preneed Funeral contract in the event the funeral firm is dishonest or goes out of business. But who wants to go through the hassle of trying to get money back? The better route is to take the time to check up on the funeral firm. You can call the North Carolina Board of Mortuary Science (919) 733-9380. Ask if the funeral firm is licensed, how long they have been in business and whether any complaints have been filed against them (NCGS 90-210.66).

Can the plan be changed after your death?

North Carolina statue states that you can cancel your contract and receive all of your money back, but suppose your heirs need to change the plan after your death because:

➢ your body is missing or cannot be recovered

➢ you were buried by another facility because your heirs were unaware of your Preneed contract

➢ you died in another country and were buried there.

Or perhaps your heirs decide on a plan different than the one you purchased? Funeral firm generally allow heirs to make changes to the plan you purchased such as:

➢ change to a more expensive plan and pay the difference

➢ change to a lesser plan and receive a refund.

You might want to check whether the contract offered by the funeral firm addresses the issue of making changes to the contract after your death.

You may wonder why anyone would think of changing the decedent's funeral plan, but consider that in today's market, it is not uncommon for a Preneed contract to cost several thousand dollars. A top end funeral complete with solid bronze casket can cost upwards of $40,000.

And there may be other motivations. Consider the case of Mona, a difficult woman with a personality that can only be described as "sour." Her husband deserted her after four years of marriage leaving her to raise their son, Lester, by herself. Once Lester was grown, Mona made it clear to him that she had done her job and now he was on his own. Lester could have used some help. He married and had three children. One of his children suffered with asthma and it was a constant struggle to keep up with the medical bills.

Mona believed in being good to herself. She did not intend to, nor did she, leave much money when she died. She knew that Lester would not be able to afford a "proper" burial for her, so she purchased a funeral plan and paid close to $18,000 for it. She was pleased when the funeral director told her that the monies would be kept safely in a trust fund until the time they were needed.

Lester was not familiar with North Carolina law, so when Mona died he asked an attorney at the Legal Aid office to determine whether the Preneed contract was revocable.

It was.

You know the ending to this story.

If you are concerned that you get the exact type of funeral that you want, with no changes, then you might consider purchasing a life insurance policy payable to your estate with instructions in your Will that you want a full probate procedure and that the money from this policy is to be used to purchase the exact type of funeral as directed in your Will. This ensures that no one can revoke your instructions, because the distribution of the insurance funds to the funeral firm is court supervised. It may be some time before your Will is probated so you need to give a copy of the Will to the funeral firm to be sure they carry out your wishes.

If you wish to purchase life insurance policy to fund your funeral and burial, but you do not want to trigger a probate procedure for a single insurance policy, then you could name a trusted family member as the beneficiary of the policy. It is important that the person who is to receive the insurance funds clearly understands why he/she is named as beneficiary of the policy. It is equally important that the beneficiary agree to use the monies for the intended purpose. It isn't so much that a family member is not trustworthy as it is that they may not understand what you intended — especially in those cases where other funds are available to pay for the funeral. Too often insurance funds are left to a sibling who then refuses to contribute to the cost of the funeral saying in effect "Dad wanted me to have this money — that's why he left it to me."

To avoid a misunderstanding, put it in writing. It need not be a formal contract. It could be something as simple as a letter to the insurance beneficiary, with copies to your next of kin. Here's an example of such a letter:

Dear Romita,

  I purchased a $20,000 insurance policy today naming you as beneficiary of the policy. As we discussed this money is to be used to pay for the following:
  - my funeral and grave site
  - my headstone
  - perpetual care for my grave
  - airfare for each of my grandchildren to attend the funeral
  - dinner for the family after the wake
  - lunch for the family after the funeral

If there is any money left over, please accept it as my thanks for all the effort spent on my behalf.
  Love,
   Dad

P.S. I am sending a copy of this letter to your brother so that he will know that all arrangements have been made.

APPOINTING A HEALTH CARE AGENT

Whether or not you arrange to pay for your burial or funeral, you need to let your next of kin know your feelings about the burial procedure. Let your family know whether you wish to be cremated or buried. If you wish to have a religious service, then let your family know the type of service and where it is to be held. Let the family know where you wish to be buried, or if you intend to be cremated, then where to place the ashes.

AUTOPSIES

As discussed in Chapter 1, some autopsies are optional. If you have strong feelings about allowing an optional autopsy or not allowing the procedure, then let your family know how you feel.

ANATOMICAL GIFTS

If you wish to make an anatomical gift, you can make that donation by completing a donor card or by letting your family know that you wish to make a donation of some or all of your body parts. Donor cards are available at your local driver's license office.

If you are aged, and in poor health, the local Organ Procurement Organization will probably not consider your body for transplantation of body parts, but you can still donate your body for education and research. If you wish to make such as donation, call or write to any of the schools mentioned on page 6. They will forward a Dedication Form to you along with information on the subject. As discussed in Chapter 1, there will be a charge to your estate for the cost of shipping to the school, so you need to give your family instructions about what to do in the event that you die far from home.

If you do not wish to make an anatomical gift, then let your family know how you feel.   Of course, there are problems with just telling someone how you feel about your burial arrangements, autopsies, and anatomical gifts:

YOU TELL THE WRONG PERSON

The person you confide in may not be present when the arrangements are made. For example, if you tell your spouse what arrangements to make then he/she may die before you do — or you could die simultaneously in a car or plane crash.

You may tell someone who does not have authority to carry out your wishes. That was the case with James. Once his wife died, he moved to a retirement community where he lived for 15 years until his death. James had two sons who lived in different states. Although he loved his sons, he had difficulty talking to either of them about serious matters. It was easier for him to talk with his friends in the retirement community. They often spoke about dying and how they felt about different burial arrangements. James would reminisce about his youth and growing up in a farming community in the plains state of Kansas. "I was happy and free. Out there you had room to breathe. It would be nice to be buried there — peaceful and spacious."

When he died, his friends told his sons about their father's desire to be buried in Kansas. They met the suggestion with scepticism and pragmatism:

"Dad didn't say anything like that to me."

"It would cost us double, if we had to arrange for burial in another state. I'm sure he didn't have that kind of expense in mind."

THE PERSON DOES NOT CARRY OUT YOUR WISHES

The person you tell may not understand what you said or perhaps they hear only what they want to hear. An example that comes to mind is the mother who constantly complained that she felt like a burden to her children. She would often say "When I die, burn my body and throw my ashes out to sea." Her children paid no attention. When she died she was given a full funeral and buried in a local cemetery. They never asked, nor did they consider, that their mother might really have wanted to be cremated.

WHO WANTS TO TALK ABOUT IT?

For many people the main problem with telling someone what to do when you die is talking about your death. It may be an uncomfortable, if not unpleasant, subject for you to bring up, and for your family to discuss. If this is the case, then consider putting the information in writing and give the instructions to the person who will have the job of carrying out your wishes.

You can legally appoint someone to carry out your wishes relating to the care of your person by signing a document called a *Health Care Power of Attorney*. North Carolina statute 32A-25 contains a statutory form that you can use to appoint a *Health Care Agent* to carry out the wishes you express in the Power of Attorney. The statutory form contains a *Living Will* that tells your Health Care Agent whether you do (or do not) want life support systems to be used in the event that you are dying and there is no hope for your recovery. You can look up the statutory form of the Power of Attorney for Health Care by going to the nearest public library or courthouse library. You can also download the form from the Internet:

 NORTH CAROLINA STATUTES
http://www.ncga.state.nc.us/

You may be thinking "Why bother with a Health Care Power of Attorney? I probably will never need anyone to assist me. And even if I did, my family will tell the doctor what I want."

That was George's thoughts exactly, even though his attorney advised him differently: "George, you are a man of substantial wealth. You should consider making provision for the care of your property in the event that you take sick. You should also appoint someone to make your medical decisions in the event that you are too sick to make them yourself. Your third wife Loretta is a lovely lady, but she and your two sons are always at odds. You should appoint someone to be your Health Care Agent."

George said he would think about it. But he didn't.

The attorney's advice turned out to be prophetic. George suffered a stroke while driving a car. His injuries from the accident combined with the severity of the stroke made for a bleak prognosis. The doctors said George would die unless they put him on a ventilator and inserted a feeding tube. Even with life support systems, it was not expected that he would ever come out of the coma.

Loretta told the doctors "Let's try everything to keep him alive."

George's sons did not see it that way. "Why torture him with needles and tubes? Let him pass on peacefully."

George never signed a Living Will, so no one knew how he felt about artificial life support systems. He never appointed a Health Care Agent, so the doctors didn't know who George would have wanted to speak on his behalf. The doctors requested that the matter be brought before the court and let a judge decide the matter.

Loretta petitioned the court to be appointed as George's guardian. So did his children. The court battle over who was to be George's guardian was bitter (and expensive). Before Loretta and George married they signed a prenuptial agreement. The agreement provided for each to give up all rights to inherit property from the other. Loretta had little money of her own. The children accused Loretta of thinking of her own best interest and not of their father. If George were to die, Loretta would be on her own.

George was a wealthy man, but he was not overly generous with his children. His sons were married and raising their own families. Without help from their father, each was struggling to support his family. Loretta accused the sons of being more concerned about their substantial inheritance than their father's well being.

The judge ruled that each of the parties had a conflict of interest and could be prejudiced by his/her own circumstances. He appointed a professional, independent, guardian to make medical decisions for George. The guardian conferred with the doctors and determined that it was futile to continue life support systems.

George died.

THE NC "IN TRUST FOR" ACCOUNT

Because of these inherent problems, you might want to hold the funds so that your beneficiary does not gain access to the monies until you die. You can do so by setting up a Trust account as allowed by North Carolina statute 53-146.2.

You can direct a financial institution to hold your account *in trust for* a beneficiary. If the account is set up according to 53-146.2 then during your lifetime:

⇨ The beneficiary does not have access to the account until you die.

⇨ You are free to add to or withdraw from the account during your lifetime.

⇨ You are free to change beneficiaries without asking the beneficiary's permission to do so.

Once you die, the bank will give the monies in the account to the named beneficiary, unless, of course, the monies are needed to pay your debts.

If it happens that the beneficiary dies before you do, then you will need to name a new beneficiary. If you do not name another beneficiary, then the monies will become part of your estate to be distributed with the rest of your property.

Everyman's Estate Plan

The first six chapters of this book describe how to wind up the affairs of the decedent. As you read those chapters, you learned about the kinds of problems that can occur when someone dies. It is relatively simple for you to make an estate plan so that your family members are not burdened with similar problems. An **estate plan** is the arranging of one's finances to reduce (if not eliminate) probate costs and estate taxes, so that your beneficiaries inherit your property quickly and at little cost.

If you think that only wealthy people need to prepare an estate plan, you are mistaken. Each year, heirs of relatively modest estates, spend thousands of dollars to settle an estate. A bit of planning could have eliminated most, if not all, of the hassle and cost suffered by those families.

The suggestions in this chapter are designed to assist the average person in preparing a practical and inexpensive estate plan, so we named this chapter EVERYMAN'S ESTATE PLAN. Once you create your own estate plan, you can rest assured that your family will not be left with more problems than happy memories of you.

TRUE OR FALSE?

(   )   If you have a Will, it must be probated.

(   )   If you don't have a Will, then probate is necessary.

(   )   Whether probate is necessary depends on how much money is involved.

If you answered true to any of the above, then go back and read chapters 5 and 6.

Hopefully the reader will forgive the authors' regression to the role of educator (or maybe pedantic). The point we were attempting to make is simply:

> Whether or not a probate procedure is necessary has nothing to do with whether there is a Will, or even how much money is involved, the determining factor is how the property is titled (owned).

Property can be held jointly with right of survivorship, or in trust (no probate) or in the decedent's name only (may need to be probated). In this chapter we explore the pros and cons of titling property in each of the three ways, beginning with holding property jointly with another.

You can arrange to have all of your bank ⟨...⟩ up so that should you die, the money goes ⟨...⟩ beneficiary. For example, suppose all you own ⟨...⟩ account and you want whatever you have in th⟨...⟩ to go to your son and daughter when you die. ⟨...⟩ think that a simple solution is to put each child's ⟨...⟩ the account, but first consider the problems ass⟨...⟩ with a joint account:

☒   **POTENTIAL LIABILITY**

If you hold a bank account jointly with one of your a⟨...⟩ children and that child is sued or gets a divorce then ⟨...⟩ child may need to disclose his/her ownership of the jo⟨...⟩ account. In such a case, you may find yourself spendi⟨...⟩ money to prove that the account was established fo⟨...⟩ convenience only and that all of the money in that accoun⟨...⟩ really belongs to you.

☒   **OVERREACHING**

If you set up a joint account with your child so that the child has authority to withdraw funds from the account, then funds may be withdrawn without your authorization. If you open a joint account with two of your children, then after your death the first child to the bank may decide to withdraw all of the money and that will, at the very least, cause hard feelings between them.

☒   **THE MINOR CHILD**

North Carolina law allows a minor to own a savings or checking account either in the child's own name or jointly with another (NCGS 54B-132, 54C-170). But if you make a minor the joint owner of your account, would you want the child to have the ability to remove money from your account. If you die, would you want the minor to be able to go to the bank and withdraw all of the money?

You can even name a minor as the beneficiary of the account. If the beneficiary is not yet 18 when you die, then the bank will give the monies in the account to the minor's court appointed guardian. If no guardian is appointed, then the bank will hold the money in a similar interest bearing account until a guardian is appointed or until the child reaches 18.

The In Trust For account solves all of the problems mentioned but it does have a drawback. North Carolina statute only allows one beneficiary for the account. If you wished to leave $50,000 to your son and daughter, then you would need to open one $25,000 account for your son and another $25,000 account for your daughter.

Later in this chapter we will discuss how you can set up a Trust Agreement so that all of your assets can be distributed from a single account to as many different beneficiaries as you wish.

REAL PROPERTY

As explained in Chapter 5, if you own real property together with another, then who will own the property upon your death depends on how the Grantee is identified on the face of the deed. If you compare the Grantee clause of the deed to the examples on pages 99 to 105 you can determine who will inherit that property should you die. If you are not satisfied with the way the property will be inherited, then you need to consult with an attorney to change the deed so that it will conform to your wishes.

If you own the property in your name only, then once you die, there will need to be a probate procedure to determine the proper beneficiary of that parcel of land. If your main objective is to avoid probate, then you can have an attorney change the deed so that once you die, the property descends to your beneficiary without the need for probate. As with bank and securities accounts there are different ways to do so, each with its own advantages and disadvantages.

JOINT OWNERSHIP

You can have your deed changed so that you and a beneficiary are joint owners with rights of survivorship. If you do so then should either of you die, the other will own the property 100%. That avoids probate but you will not be able to sell that property during your lifetime without the beneficiary's permission. And if the beneficiary gives permission and the property is sold, the beneficiary will have the right to half of the proceeds of the sale.

GIFT OF HOMESTEAD

Some people think it a good idea to simply transfer their homestead to their children to avoid probate, but continue to live there. But this just creates a new set of problems:

⊠ RISK OF LOSS

If you transfer your homestead to a beneficiary it could be lost if the beneficiary runs into serious financial difficulties or gets sued. This is especially a risk if your child is a professional (doctor, nurse, accountant, financial planner, attorney, etc.). If your child is found to be personally liable for damages, then the house could become part of the settlement of that law suit.

If your child is (or gets) married, then this complicates matters more so. If the child is divorced, the property will certainly be included as part of the settlement agreement. This may be to your child's detriment because the child may need to share the value of the property with his ex-spouse. If you do not transfer the property, then it cannot become part of the marital equation.

⊠ POSSIBLE LOSS OF GOVERNMENT BENEFITS

If you transfer property, then depending upon the value of the transfer, you could be disqualified from receiving Medicaid or Supplemental Security Income ("SSI") benefits for up to 3 years from the date of transfer. The federal and state rules that determine the period of ineligibility are complex. If nursing care may be an issue in the future, then it is best to consult with an Elder Law attorney to prepare a Medicaid Estate Plan.

☒ LOSS OF HOMESTEAD CREDITOR PROTECTION

Up to $10,000 of the value of your homestead is protected from your creditors. This means that if a creditor forces the sale of the property then you get to keep $10,000 of the proceeds of the sale (NCGS 1C-1601). Of course this does not apply to someone who has a mortgage on your property. Ten thousand dollars is not much creditor protection. The more important protection is that offered to your spouse and minor children should you die. As explained on page 87, your creditors cannot force the sale of the property until your children are adults and your spouse either remarries or dies. If you make a gift of your homestead, then you lose your creditor protection for yourself and for your spouse and minor children.

☒ POSSIBLE CAPITAL GAINS TAX

If you gift your homestead to your child and continue to live there until you die, then when the child sells the property there might be a capital gains tax. The child will be taxed on the increase in value from the day you bought the property. If you don't transfer your home and the child inherits the property, he/she inherits it at the market value as of your date of death. The child can sell the property at that time without any tax consequence.

☒ POSSIBLE GIFT TAX

If the value of the transfer is worth more than $10,000 you need to file a gift tax return. For Federal tax purposes, you can give up to $675,000 during your lifetime in excess of the $10,000 per person per year (see page 38). For North Carolina tax purposes you can give a total of $100,000 during your lifetime over and above the $10,000 per person per year. If you make a gift of a your homestead, you may need to pay a North Carolina gift tax.

☎ LAWYER	OUT OF STATE PROPERTY

Each state is in charge of the way property located in that state is transferred. If you own property in another state (or country) then you need to consult with an attorney in that state (or country) to determine how that property will be transferred to your beneficiaries once you die. Most state laws are similar to North Carolina, namely, property held as **JOINT TENANTS WITH RIGHTS OF SURVIVORSHIP** or a **LIFE ESTATE INTEREST** go to your beneficiary without the need for probate.

If you own property in another state in your name only, or as a **TENANT IN COMMON**, or if you hold property jointly with your spouse in a community property state, then a probate procedure may need to be held in that state. If it is necessary for your heirs to have probate procedure in North Carolina, then they will need an ancillary (secondary) procedure in the state in which the property is located. This could have the effect of doubling the cost of probate to your heirs.

Still another problem is the matter of taxes. In addition to paying for a second probate procedure, your heirs may need to pay inheritance taxes in the state where the property is located as well as in North Carolina. Your heirs may need to file a tax return in two states. This may double the cost of the accounting fees.

You may wish to consult with an attorney for suggestions about how to set up your estate plan to avoid such problems.

A TRUST MAY BE THE SOLUTION (or not)

As we have seen, many of the ways to avoid probate involve methods with undesirable trade-offs. One way to avoid some of these potential problems is to set up a **Inter Vivos Trust** (also known as a **Living Trust**). A Living Trust is operational during your lifetime and can be used upon your death, to distribute your property, as you wish, and without the need for probate. You may have been encouraged to set up such a trust by your financial planner, or attorney, or accountant. Even people of modest means are being encouraged by these professionals to use a trust as the basis of their estate plan. But trusts have their pros and cons. But before getting into that, let's first discuss what a trust is and how it works:

SETTING UP A TRUST

To create a trust, an attorney prepares the trust document in accordance with the client's needs and desires. The person who signs the document as the **Trustor** or **Settlor**. If the person who creates the trust also funds the trust, then he is referred to as the **Grantor**. We will refer to the Inter Vivos Trust as the "Living Trust" and the person setting up the trust as the "Grantor."

The trust document identifies who is to be the Trustee (manager) of property placed in the trust. Usually the Grantor appoints himself as Trustee so that he is in total control of property that he places into the Trust. The trust document also names a Successor Trustee who will take over the management of the trust property should the Trustee become disabled or die.

Once the trust document is properly signed, the Grantor transfers property into the trust. The Grantor does this by changing the name on the account from his individual name to his name as Trustee. For example, if ELAINE RICHARDS sets up a trust naming herself as trustee, and she wishes to place her bank account into the trust then all she need do is instruct the bank to change the name on the account from   ELAINE RICHARDS to:

ELAINE RICHARDS, TRUSTEE of the ELAINE RICHARDS
TRUST AGREEMENT DATED JANUARY 12, 2000.

Once the change is made, all the money in the bank account becomes trust property. Elaine (wearing her trustee hat) has total control of the account, taking money out, and putting money in, as she sees fit.

The trust document states how the trust property is to be managed during Elaine's lifetime. If the trust is a Revocable Living Trust, then it will say that Elaine has the power to terminate the trust at any time and have all trust property returned to her. Should Elaine become disabled or die, then her Successor Trustee will take possession of the trust funds and manage (or distribute them) according to the directions Elaine gave in the trust document. If the trust says that once Elaine dies, the property is to be given to her beneficiary, then the Successor Trustee will do so; and in most cases without a probate procedure. If the trust directs the Successor Trustee to hold property in trust to care for a member of the Elaine's family, then the Successor Trustee will do so.

THE GOOD PART
Setting up a trust has many good features.

☆ AVOID GUARDIANSHIP PROCEDURES
If you become disabled or too aged to handle your finances, then you do not need to worry about who takes care of your finances. Your trust appoints a Successor Trustee to take over the care of your trust if you are unable to do so. If you do not have a trust and you become incapacitated, a court may need to appoint a guardian to care for your property. The cost to establish and maintain the guardianship is charged to you. Guardianship procedures are expensive and once established cannot be terminated unless you die or are restored to health.

☆ AVOID PROBATE
Probate procedures can be very expensive. Both the Personal Representative and his attorney are entitled to reasonable fees. It may be necessary to hire accountants and appraisers, as well. If you have property in two states, then two probate procedures may be necessary (one in each state) and that could be costly. If the trust is properly drafted and your property placed into the trust, you may be able to avoid probate altogether.

Incidentally, if you are married, then your spouse has the right to a life estate in the homestead should you die (see page 123). If you wish to put any real property into your trust, then your spouse must agree to the transfer and must sign the deed to place the property into the trust (NCGS 39-7(a)).

☆ PRIVACY

Your Living Trust is a private document. No one but your trustee and your beneficiaries need ever read it. If you leave property in a Will and there is a probate procedure, the Will is filed with the court. The Will becomes a public document. Anyone can go to the courthouse, read your Will and see who you did (or did not) provide for in your Will (NCGS 31-20).

☆ CARE FOR A CHILD OR FAMILY MEMBER

You can make provision in your trust to care the finances of a child or a family member after you die. If your family member is immature or a born spender, you can set up a Spendthrift Trust to protect him/her from squandering the inheritance. You can direct your Successor Trustee to use trust funds to pay for the family member's health care, education or living expenses, and nothing more.

☆ TAX SAVINGS:

There can be substantial Estate tax savings if you are married and you and your spouse each set up your own trust. For example, suppose you and your spouse together have an estate worth one million dollars. You can each set up your own trust with $500,000. Each trust can provide that if one of you dies, the surviving spouse can use the income from the deceased partner's trust for living expenses. Once the second partner dies, all of the monies in the two trusts can be distributed, with no estate taxes due on either trust. By doing this, you each take advantage of your own Estate and Gift Tax Exclusion. If you don't separate the funds and one of you dies, the surviving spouse has only his own Estate and Gift Tax Exclusion. If the surviving spouse has one million dollars and the Exclusion amount $675,000, then the beneficiaries will pay taxes on anything over $675,000. If the tax rate is 37% then the beneficiaries will pay 37% of $325,000 or $120,250 in Estate taxes.

☆ LEASE A SAFE DEPOSIT BOX AS TRUSTEE

You can lease a safe deposit box as Trustee of your trust. Your can set up the lease so that your Successor Trustee has equal access to the box. If you do not wish your Successor Trustee to have access to the box while you are able to conduct business, you can keep both keys to the box in your possession. In the event you become incapacitated, you can arrange to make the key available to your Successor Trustee at that time.

THE PROBLEMS

A trust is an excellent estate planning tool, but there are some things you need to consider:

⊠ COMPLEXITY

A trust is a fairly complex document, often over 20 pages long. It needs to be that long because you are establishing a vehicle for taking care of your property during your lifetime, as well as after your death. The trust usually is written in "legalese," so it may take you considerable time and effort to understand it. It is important to have your trust document prepared by an attorney who has the patience to work with you until you fully understand each paragraph of the document and are satisfied that this is what you want.

⊠ COST

Because of the thoroughness of the document and the fact that it is custom designed for you, a trust will cost much more to draft than a simple Will. In addition to the initial cost of the trust, it can be expensive to maintain the trust should you become disabled or die. Your Successor Trustee has the right to charge for his duties as trustee, as well as to charge for any specialized services performed

If you choose an attorney to be Successor Trustee, the attorney has the right to charge to manage the trust, and also charge for any legal work he performs (NCGS 32-51). A financial institution can charge to serve as Successor Trustee, and also charge to manage the trust portfolio. Regardless of whether you choose a professional or a family member to be Successor Trustee, you need to determine what will be charged to manage the trust.

Once you agree to the amount to be paid, you can make a provision in the trust for that amount to be paid to your Successor Trustee. If you do not make a provision for fees in your trust document, then North Carolina statute 32-50 has a schedule of fees that can be charged by the Trustee. The fee schedule sets compensation for the annual gross income of the trust and for compensation on the principal value of personal property (securities, bank accounts, etc.).

Compensation for income starts at 5% for the first $5,000 and graduates downward to 2% on all income over $50,000. Compensation on the Trust principal begins at 0.4% on the first $25,000 and graduates down to 0.05% on amounts over $200,000. If the Trustee does work beyond the usual duties of a Trustee, he can ask the Clerk of the Superior Court to award additional fees. The Clerk can award up to 5% of the gross income and .5% of all of the trust principal (both real and personal property).

⊠ TAXES MAY STILL BE A PROBLEM:
While the Grantor is operating the trust as Trustee, all of
the property held in a Revocable Living Trust is taxed as if
the Grantor were holding that property in his/her own
name. If the value of the trust property exceeds the Estate
and Gift Tax Exclusion amount (see page 37 for the value),
then unless the Grantor takes some other, more advanced,
Estate Planning strategy, taxes will be due and owing
once the Grantor dies.

⊠ NO CREDITOR PROTECTION
Because property held in a Revocable Living Trust is
freely accessible to the Grantor, it is likewise accessible
to his creditors both before and after the Grantor's death.
If the Grantor dies owing money then the Personal
Representative can request that trust funds can be used to
pay for those debts (NCGS 28A-15-10).

⊠ PROBATE MIGHT STILL BE NECESSARY
The trust only works for those items that you place in the
trust. If you have property that is held jointly with
another, then when you die, that property will go to the
joint owner and not to the trust. If you purchase a security
in your name only, and forget to put it in your trust, there
will need to be a probate procedure to determine the
beneficiary of that security.

MAYBE PROBATE ISN'T ALL THAT BAD

As explained, if you hold all of your property in trust or jointly with another, you may be able to avoid probate and have your property go directly to your heirs, but you may have reason not to choose either of these methods. Maybe you don't have money at this time to pay an attorney to set up a trust. Maybe you do not want to hold your money jointly with anyone because you are concerned about losing your independence or maybe you are concerned about keeping your money secure.

If you arrange all of your finances so that the money goes directly to a few beneficiaries, then this plan may not be as flexible as you wish. This is especially the case if you wish to give gifts to several charities or to minor children instead of just one or two beneficiaries. For example, if you hold all of your property so that it goes directly to your child without the need for probate, then your child becomes the legal owner of your property as of your date of death. If you tell your child to use some of that money as a donation to your church and some of it for your grandchild's education, then that puts an unreasonable burden on your child because you were not specific as to exactly how much of that money you wished to be donated. Also you did not say how the money is to be used for the child. Is the money for tuition only? Can the money be used to pay the child's living expenses?

Even if you give your child specific instructions about how the money is to be spent, and even if your child is honorable and with the best intentions, it may be that your grandchild get none of the money, because your child is sued or falls upon hard times and is forced to use that money to pay debts. If you keep your property in your own name and leave a Will giving a certain amount of money for your grandchild, then he/she will know exactly how much money you left and the purpose of that gift.

YOUR WILL — YOUR WAY

Many people decide that the Will is the best route to go but do not act upon it, thinking it unnecessary to prepare a Will until they are very old and about to die. But according to reports published by the National Center for Health Statistics (a division of the U.S. Department of Health and Human Services) 2 of every 10 people who die in any given year are under the age of 60. Twenty percent may seem like a small number until it hits close to home as it did with a young couple. The couple was having difficulty conceiving a child. They went from doctor to doctor until they met someone just beginning his practice. With his knowledge of the latest advances in medicine, he was able to help them. The birth of their child was a moment of joy and gratitude. They asked a nurse to take a picture of them all together — the happy couple, the newborn child and the doctor who made it all happen. Happiness radiated from the picture, but one of them would be dead within six months.

You might think it was the child. An infant's life is so fragile. SIDS and all manner of childhood diseases can threaten a little one.
But no, he grew up to be a healthy young man.

If you looked at the picture, you might guess the husband. Overweight and stressed out; his ruddy complexion suggested high blood pressure. He looked like a typical heart- attack-prone type A personality.
No, he was fine and went on to enjoy raising his son.

Probably the wife. She had such a difficult time with the pregnancy and the delivery was especially hard. Perhaps it was all too much for her.
No, she recovered and later had two more children.

It was the doctor who was killed in a three car collision.

Though we all agree that one never knows, still people put off making a Will figuring that if they die before getting around to it, North Carolina law will take over and their property will be distributed in the manner that they would have wanted anyway. The problem with that logic is the complexity of the Laws of Descent and Distribution. If you are survived by a spouse, child, parent or sibling, then it isn't too difficult to figure out who will inherit your property. If none of these survive you, the ultimate beneficiary of your property may not be the person you would have chosen, had you taken the time to do so.

You may think there is no rush to make a Will because you have arranged your finances so that your property will go to whom you wish, automatically, and without the need for probate. But consider that if you die as a result of an accident, someone will need to be appointed as your Personal Representative to sue on behalf of your estate. It is better to leave a Will so that you can say who will be in charge of handling your affairs once you die. If you don't have a Will and a probate procedure is necessary then the Clerk of the Superior Court will choose someone for you (see Page 145).

Still another benefit to making a Will is that you can make provision for who will get your personal property, including your car. Without a Will, your Personal Representative gets to make these decisions.

For most of us, the primary benefit of a Will is that you can rest assured that your property will be distributed according to your directions. The court will supervise the distribution of property that is titled in your name only. Any deviation from the instructions given in your Will can be made only for good cause and with court approval.

MAKE A GIFT OF YOUR CAR

If you hold a car jointly with rights of survivorship, then should you die all the surviving joint owner need do is go to the Department of Motor Vehicles and have the car transferred to their name only.

CAVEAT: If you and your spouse own a car as "husband and wife," then in North Carolina, that does not mean that your spouse automatically owns the car should you die. If you want your spouse to own the car upon your death, then you need to have title to the car state that there are *rights of survivorship.*

If title to your car is in your name only and you are married, then it is relatively simple for your spouse to use a Small Estate Affidavit to transfer the car upon your death provided your car is worth $20,000 or less. If you are not married, then the car can be transferred with a Small Estate Affidavit, but the value of the transfer cannot be greater than $10,000 (see Page 129). If the value of your car exceeds these values, a full probate procedure will be necessary.

You may be thinking that it is just as easy to hold the car jointly with rights of survivorship and avoid all the hassle. But the problem with joint ownership of a motor vehicle is liability. If either owner is in an accident with the car, then both may be liable for any damage that is done. If you are single, the better route may be to hold title to the car in your name only and make a gift of the car in your Will to the person of your choice. If you do not make a specific gift of your car in your Will, then it becomes part of your Probate Estate and your Personal Representative will decide whether to sell the car or give it to a beneficiary as part of the beneficiary's share of the estate.

FOR PET LOVERS

A woman died at peace,
leaving her fortune
and care of her cat to her niece.
Alas, the fortune and the cat
Soon disappeared after that.

You could make provision in your Will for the care of your pet, but the moral of the above limerick, is that leaving your money to someone to do the job may not be the best route to go.

   TRUST FOR CARE OF PET

If you are serious about caring for your pet after your death, you can employ an attorney to set up a separate trust for the care of your pet, or you can have the attorney include a trust provision in your Will (NCGS 36A-147).

The trust will direct the trustee to pay sufficient monies to a custodian for the care of the pet. You also need to name a beneficiary (a person or charitable organization) to receive whatever may remain in the trust after the pet dies.

If you intend the trustee to also serve as custodian of the pet, then you can ask the beneficiary to regularly check on the pet to see to it that the pet is treated humanely, if not benevolently.

CARE OF PETS (Continued)

If you don't have the resources to set up a trust to care for your pet, you can still ask a fellow pet lover to care for the animal. If no one among your circle of family and friends is able to do so, then ask your pet's veterinarian to consider starting an "Orphaned Pet Service" to assist in finding new homes for pets who lose their owners. It is good public relations and a potential source of income. You can make provision in your Will to pay the Vet to care for the pet until a suitable family can be found. This is a more humane approach than the, all too common practice, of putting a pet to sleep" rather than have the pet suffer the loss of its master. And in at least one case, that reasoning backfired.

Eleanor always had a pet in the house. After her husband died, her two poodles were her constant companions. When Eleanor became ill with cancer, she worried about what would happen to her "buddies" if she died. She finally decided it best to have her family put them to sleep when she died.

Eleanor endured surgery, chemotherapy, radiation therapy, and even some holistic remedies, but she continued to go downhill. Eleanor's family came in to visit her at the hospital to say their last good-byes. She was so ill, she didn't even recognize them. No one thought she could last the day. Because the family was from out of state, and time short, they decided to put the pets to sleep so they need only take care of the funeral arrangements when she died. To everyone's surprise, Eleanor rallied. She lived two more long, lonely years.

Eleanor often said she wished they had put her to sleep instead of her buddies.

PROVIDING FOR A MINOR CHILD

Parents have a special responsibility. They need to make provision for the care of their child in the event they both die or become incapacitated before the child is grown. It is unusual for a child to lose both parents, but it does happen, and parents need to provide for this possibility.

A child must be cared for in two ways, the **person** of the child and **estate** of the child. To care for the person of the child, someone must be in charge of the child's everyday living, not only food and shelter but to provide social, ethical and religious training. Someone must have legal authority to make medical decisions and see to the child's education.

To care for the child's estate, someone must take charge of monies left to the child. That person is responsible to see that the monies are used for the care of the child and that anything left over is preserved until the child becomes an adult.

If one parent dies, then it is the right (and duty) of the surviving parent to care for the child. If both parents die or are incapacitated and unable to care for their child, then the Clerk of the Superior Court will appoint someone as Guardian of the person of the child, and someone to be the Guardian of the estate of the child, or a General Guardian to care for the person and the estate of the child.

APPOINTING A GUARDIAN FOR THE CHILD

The child's parent is the one best suited to choose a guardian for that child. It is relatively simple for a parent to appoint someone to be Guardian of his/her minor child, in the event of the incapacity or death of both parents. All the parent need do is to put a provision in his/her Will nominating someone to be Guardian of the child's person or Guardian of the child's estate or a General Guardian to care for the child's person and property.

The person nominated as Guardian can assume the care of the child upon the death of the last surviving parent, but the Clerk of the Superior Court needs to appoint that person as the child's legal Guardian. In making the appointment, the Clerk will be guided by the choice made by the parent in his/her Will. If the child's parents die in close proximity and each have a Will naming a different guardian, then the Clerk will be guided by the Will with the latest date.

Although the Clerk is guided by the parent's choice of Guardian, the Clerk's primary consideration in making the appointment is the best interest of the child. If the Clerk determines that person chosen by the parent is not qualified to be the child's Guardian, the Clerk will appoint someone who is (NCGS 35A-1225).

LEAVING PROPERTY FOR THE CHILD

As any parent is well aware, it is expensive to raise a child. People that you might consider to be the best choice to serve as your child's Guardian might not be able to do so unless you leave sufficient monies to pay for the care of the child. If you are a person of limited finances, then consider purchasing a term life insurance policy on your life and/or on the life of the other parent of the child. If you can only afford one policy, then insure the life of the parent who contributes most to the support of the child.

Term insurance policies are relatively inexpensive if you limit the term to just that period of time until your child becomes an adult. Some companies offer a combination of term life and disability insurance. As with any other purchase, it is important to comparison shop to obtain the best price for the coverage.

If you are married to the parent of your child, then the beneficiary of the term insurance policy can be your spouse with your child as an alternate beneficiary. Married or single, you can name your child as the primary beneficiary of the policy. If you name the child as beneficiary of the policy that is no more than $20,000 in value, and you die before the child is 21, then the insurance company will either turn over the funds to the child's guardian or to a financial institution as Custodian Trustee (NCGS 33B-1(6), 33B-5). If the amount is over $20,000, a guardian of the property, will need to be appointed to take custody of the insurance proceeds. The judge usually appoints the surviving parent as Guardian of the child's property. The court will not allow the Guardian to spend any of the insurance funds without court approval. The court will require that the guardian give the court an accounting to be sure that the monies are being preserved for the benefit of the child.

If the other parent is able to care for the child, then it is best to avoid guardianship proceedings because they can be time-consuming and expensive. If you are planning to leave more than $20,000, then the better route might be to name a Custodian for the insurance funds under the North Carolina Uniform Transfers to Minors Act.

THE NORTH CAROLINA UNIFORM TRANSFERS TO MINORS ACT

You can appoint a person or a financial institution to be the Custodian of the insurance funds until your child is an adult. For example, you can identify the beneficiary of your life insurance policy as follows:

> Friendly Trust Company as Custodian for FRANK BARRY, JR. under the NORTH CAROLINA UNIFORM TRANSFERS TO MINORS ACT.

You can elect to have the Custodian give the money to the child at any age between 18 and 21. If you choose 21, and you die after your child reaches that age, then the insurance proceeds will be turned over the child. If you die before the child 21, the Custodian will hold and manage the account until the child reaches 21. The Custodian can deliver or spend as much of the money for the child's care as they think advisable. If there is a disagreement about using the funds, then the child's parent or guardian (or the child himself if he is 14 or older) can ask a court to order that the bank use monies for the child's care.

The same law can be used if you wish to name a minor as beneficiary of a bank account, life insurance policy, and even real property. The Custodian has the right to charge a reasonable fee for their efforts, so before making the appointment, you need to find out how the Custodian intends to manage the funds and the estimated charge for doing so (NCGS 33A-3, 33A-9, 33A-14, 33A-15, 33A-20)).

 **A TRUST FOR THE CHILD**

If you have sufficient monies to care for your child until adulthood, then consult with an attorney about setting up a trust for the child or drafting a Will with a trust provision in the event you die before the child is grown. The only problem with having a trust included in your Will is that the trust is funded by your Probate Estate; and as such may increase the cost of probate. If you have a significant amount of money, the better route might be to set up a Revocable Living Trust. You can fund the trust while you are alive and bypass probate altogether.

The person you name as Successor Trustee will handle the trust funds should you die before the child reaches maturity. You can name the other parent as your Trustee, or if you wish, you can appoint a financial institution to manage the trust funds. If you do not appoint the other parent as Trustee, then that parent still has the right, and duty, to care for the child. If you instruct the Trustee to use trust funds for the child's support and maintenance, then the Trustee can set up a payment schedule with the parent to use the funds for everyday necessities.

If you instruct the Trustee to keep all of the funds invested until the child reaches maturity, then the Trustee will do so and distribute the trust funds directly to the child at whatever age you specify in the trust document.

PROVIDING FOR THE STEPCHILD

Perhaps the reason that the story of Cinderella has such universal appeal is that many stepchildren, at one point or another, feel left out. The law seems to reinforce that perception. If you have a stepchild, you and not the child, have priority in determining whether an autopsy should be performed or an anatomical gift made. Should your spouse die without a Will, then you have priority over your stepchild to be appointed as Personal Representative. If all of your spouse's property is held jointly with you, then should your spouse die first, your stepchild will be left nothing. If your spouse takes ill, generally the doctors will consult with you and not the stepchild (NCGS 28A-4-1, 130A-398(6) 130-404).

Of course, allowing you to make medical decisions and inherit property must be a decision that is agreeable to your spouse. If your spouse wants the child to have primary authority to make medical decisions, then your spouse can sign a Power of Attorney For Health Care and appoint the child (and not you) as Health Care Agent. If your spouse wants his/her child to inherit property, then your spouse can arrange his/her finances so that the child will inherit the property.

Hopefully, your spouse will consult with an estate planning attorney who can explain the best way to achieve that goal, else that intent could be thwarted and the child end up with less than your spouse intends as was the case in the example given on page 121.

PROVIDING FOR THE ADULT CHILD

It isn't just stepchildren who can be left out if no provision is made. Even children from a long-standing marriage can be cut off against the wishes of a parent. A parent may assume that all of their children will be treated equally once they are both gone, but consider that the last to die is the one who gets to decide "who gets what." That was the case with Joan and Herbert. They were a devoted couple, married over forty years. Herb was the breadwinner, but he was content to let Joan handle all of the finances.

Joan wanted to be sure that each of their three daughters would always have a decent place to live. They purchased a three story house and each of the daughters moved into a different floor of the home. It was their parents' intent that once they were both gone, the daughters would inherit and occupy the building.

The couple held everything jointly. When Joan died, all of their property, including the home, was owned by Herbert. The grief suffered by Herbert at his wife's passing was more than he could bear. He alternated between sadness, despair and anger.

His middle daughter took the brunt of his anger. Their relationship had always been strained. She felt she could never live up to her father's expectations. She was not the cute baby of the family as was her younger sister. She was not the eldest daughter who always seemed to make her Dad proud. He always made her feel that she was a disappointment to him. Once her mother died, she had no one left to buffer the relationship with her father.

Soon after Joan's death, Herbert had an attorney draft a Will leaving all to his eldest and youngest daughter. None of the children knew what he had done.

Herbert decided to take a trip to Europe to try to escape the pain of his mourning. When he was in France, he suffered a heart attack and died. He died within 6 months of Joan's death.

If he had returned from Europe, Herbert may have reconciled with his daughter, but as it happened, there was no time for them to develop a better relationship.

With both their parents gone, the eldest and youngest daughter decided to sell the home. The youngest sister offered some of the proceeds to middle daughter. The middle daughter refused the offer with unkind words. Being offered less than her one-third share, meant to her that her sisters approved of their father's action. It was as if she were being disinherited all over again.

It was unfortunate that Joan's best plans were thwarted. They didn't have to be. She and Herbert could have kept a life estate in the property with the remainder going to all three girls. That would have ensured that each daughter received an equal inheritance. More importantly, the family would not have been torn by the hurt and anger that was more a product of a husband's grief than the absence of a father's love.

PROVIDING FOR INCAPACITY

As the life expectancy of the population increases, so does the percentage of the population who suffer from debilitating diseases such Alzheimer's and Parkinsons'. As a person ages, his chances for suffering dementia as a result of a stroke or other debilitating diseases increases. It is estimated that more than 50% of the population who are 85 or older, suffer from some degree of dementia.

If you are concerned that you may become disabled in the future, you need to consider who will care for your property and who will take care of your person. You can have an attorney prepare a trust. You can be trustee of the funds while you have capacity. Once you can no longer do so, then the person you name as Successor Trustee will take over.

If you do not have sufficient assets to justify the cost of employing an attorney to draft a trust, you can appoint someone to be your Agent to care for your property and make your medical decisions in the event of your incapacity by signing a *Power of Attorney*.

If you think you may just need help in paying for your bills, then you can open a *Personal Agency* account. In some states it is called a *Convenience* account. The person you name as your Agent can sign checks and make deposits into the account on your behalf. Once you die the Agent no longer can transact business with your account. All the money in the account becomes part of your Probate Estate, to be distribute according to your Will, or inherited by your heirs under the North Carolina laws of Descent and Distribution (NCGS 53-146.3).

 **LAWYER** # PROVIDING FOR THE CARETAKER

If you are the caretaker or legal guardian of someone who is incapacitated, then in addition to preparing your own estate plan, you need to be concerned about who will care for the incapacitated person should something happen to you. Someone will need to make medical decisions for the incapacitated person and see to it that he/she is properly housed and fed.

APPOINTMENT OF A SUCCESSOR CARETAKER

Often a family member will agree to take responsibility for the care of an incapacitated person in the event that the caretaker dies. But perhaps no one wants the job, or the opposite case, too many want to have control. For example, if a parent is incapacitated, one child may want the parent to remain at home with the assistance of a home health care worker. Another child may think the best place for the parent is an assisted living facility with 24 hour care. The caretaker spouse may be concerned that a tug-of-war will erupt once he dies.

In such case, the caretaker should consult with an attorney to ensure future care for the incapacitated person. The attorney may suggest establishing a trust or having a legal guardian appointed for the incapacitated person while the parent/caretaker is alive. Once the guardianship is in place, the court will continue to supervise the care of the incapacitated person until he/she dies.

 **LAWYER** ## A SPECIAL NEEDS TRUST FOR THE INCAPACITATED

If a person is incapacitated, both the federal and state government provide assistance with programs such as social security disability benefits and custodial nursing home care under the Medicaid program. The family often supplements the government program by providing for the incapacitated person's *special needs*, such as clothing, hobbies, special education, outings to a movie or a sports event — things that give the incapacitated person some quality of life.

To be eligible for government assistance programs the incapacitated person must be essentially without funds. Caretakers fear that leaving money to the incapacitated person in a will or trust will disqualify him/her from further government assistance. Understanding this dilemma, both the state and the federal government have passed laws allowing caretakers to set up a *Special Needs* trust with the incapacitated as the beneficiary of the trust (NCGS 36A-59.10). One type of Special Needs Trust is the *Disability Trust* as authorized by 42 U.S.C.1382c(a)(3). A trustee is appointed to use trust funds to provide for the special needs of the incapacitated person. If any trust funds are left after he/she dies, then those funds must be used to reimburse the state for monies spent on behalf of the incapacitated person.

There are other types of special needs trusts that are allowed under the law. An experienced Elder Law attorney can explain what options are available and can assist the family member in preparing a Will or trust that will provide for the incapacitated person's special needs once the family member dies.

ARRANGING TO PAY BILLS

When people draft a Will they are more concerned about giving their possessions away than they are about taking into account what they actually have to give. This was the case with Larry. He had no family to speak of. After his wife died, he bought a condominium in Springfield. Over the years, he developed a close network of friends. They became his family. Larry did not have much money. His car was leased. He had a mortgage on the condominium. He wanted his friends to know how much they meant to him so he had a Will drafted giving all he owned to five close friends.

The friends appreciated the gesture but the probate procedure turned out to be a nightmare. They had to keep current the mortgage payments and the maintenance fees until the condominium was sold. Because Larry left little cash, this money had to come out of the beneficiaries' pockets. Two were living on their social security income and they had to borrow money from the others to contribute to their share of the upkeep.

The beneficiaries had no money to settle the lease on the car. Even if they did, they decided that there was no point in doing so because the amount needed to obtain clear title was greater than the current market value of the car. The beneficiaries decided not to make any further payment and they returned the car to the leasing agent. Their decision turned out to be a losing proposition. The leasing agent took the car, sold it and then sued the estate for the balance of the monies owed on the lease.

Because the beneficiaries had to quickly liquidate the estate, the condominium sold for less than it would have had they the time, energy and resources to fix it up. After they settled with the leasing agent, paid off the funeral expenses, mortgage, and probate fees there was only a few hundred dollars left. That was a lot of work and stress for nothing.

The pity was that Larry could have arranged his finances so that his beneficiaries were not burdened by his debt. He could have taken out mortgage insurance as part of the loan package. In most cases the cost of the insurance is nominal and is included as part of the monthly mortgage payment.

Larry could have done the same when he leased the car. Most leasing contracts offer term life insurance as an option. The cost of such insurance depends on the age of the person, the term of the loan and the amount of monies owed, but the premium paid each month is just a small fraction of the loan payment.

Even if Larry just arranged for payment of one of these debts, his beneficiaries would have come away with the gift that Larry intended, instead of the headache that they inherited.

PROVIDE FOR CREDIT CARD DEBT

If you have significant credit card debt, you need to consider how that debt will be paid once you die. Most credit card companies offer insurance policies and include the premium as part of your monthly payment. If you have such insurance, then should you die, any outstanding balance is paid. It benefits the credit card company to offer life insurance as part of the credit package, because they are assured of prompt payment should the borrower die. However, if you have little or no assets and no one other than yourself is liable to pay the debt, you may have no incentive to pay for insurance that can only benefit the lender.

As discussed in Chapters 2 and 4, if you hold a credit card jointly with another person, both of you are equally liable to pay the debt. If one of you dies, the other is responsible to pay the bill regardless of who ran up the bill. If paying that bill could be a struggle for the surviving debtor, then the better route to go is for each of you to have your own credit card.

Still another reason not to hold a joint credit card is that each of you can establish your own line of credit. This is especially important if you are married and one of you is retired or has been out of the job market for any period of time. Should the breadwinner die, it may be difficult for the surviving partner to establish credit if he/she has no recent work record It is easier for the unemployed spouse to establish a line of credit when he/she is married to someone who is working.

PURCHASE LIFE INSURANCE

The good part of purchasing loan insurance — be it credit card insurance, mortgage insurance or car insurance, is that you can usually purchase the insurance without taking a medical examination. The down side is that such insurance may be more expensive than a life insurance policy. If you are in fairly good health, consider taking out a life insurance policy to cover all of your outstanding loans. The cost of the single life insurance policy may be significantly less than purchasing separate loan insurance policies.

The estate planning strategy of purchasing life insurance to pay off all of your loans works best if you are married and your spouse is jointly liable for your debts. If you name your spouse as beneficiary of the life insurance policy, then he/she can use the life insurance funds to pay off all monies owed. If you name someone as beneficiary and that person has no legal obligation to pay your debts, then none of your creditors can force your beneficiary to use any part of those funds to pay your debts

If you want the insurance funds used to pay your debts, then this may not be the way to go. But, if you want to be sure that someone receives money for their care after you are gone, and you do not want those funds reduced by the cost of probate or to pay off your debts, then this strategy should accomplish your goal, with one caveat. If you purchased the insurance policy at a time when you owed a significant amount of money, and if your creditor can prove that you purchased the policy with the intent to defraud your creditor, then a court can order that the insurance proceeds be used to pay your debt (NCGS 58-58-115).

Which brings us to the issue of life insurance — should you have it? How much is enough? The answer to these questions depends on the "sleep at night" factor, namely how much insurance do you need to make you not worry about insurance coverage when you go to sleep at night? It is often more an emotional than a financial issue.

Some people have an "every man for himself" attitude and are content to have no life insurance at all. Others worry about how their loved ones will manage if they are not around to support them. The same person may have different thoughts about insurance coverage as the circumstances of their life changes — from no coverage in their bachelor days to more-than-enough coverage in their child rearing days to just-enough-to-bury-me in their senior years. Insurance companies recognize that people's needs change over the years. Many companies offer flexible insurance coverage. As with any consumer item, it is a good idea to shop around.

In addition to life insurance, you might want to consider long-term health care insurance. Your best estate plan could be sabotaged by a lengthy, or debilitating illness. If you are poor, long-term nursing care may not be of concern to you, because all your needs should be covered under Medicaid. If you are very wealthy, you may not worry because you have more than enough money to pay for your care. But the rest of us need to think about ways to provide for long-term health care. An experienced Elder law attorney can suggest an estate plan that will preserve your assets in the event of a lengthy illness.

If long-term care insurance is part of your estate plan, then you need to consider the many plans available. You can get the publication A SHOPPER'S GUIDE TO LONG-TERM CARE INSURANCE from the National Association of Insurance Commissioners by calling (816) 842-3600.

ANNUITIES TO SPREAD THE INHERITANCE

Most beneficiaries go through their inheritance within two years. For many, the reason the money is gone so soon, is that there just wasn't much money to inherit in the first place. But for others, it's a spending frenzy.

People's spending habits remain much the same throughout their lifetime. Some people are squirrels, always saving for the winter. For others, it's:

Earn-A-Penny   Spend-A-Penny

Most of us fall somewhere in between. We are not extravagant in our spending habits, yet it is a struggle to save. But why should we struggle to purchase an insurance policy if the intended beneficiary will spend it in a few months?

If you want to leave an insurance policy benefit to someone you love, but the intended beneficiary is immature, or a born spendthrift, then a simple solution to the problem may be to purchase an annuity rather than life insurance.

An annuity is a type of insurance policy that can be set up so that your beneficiary (the *annuitant*) receives money on a monthly, or yearly basis, rather than a single lump sum payment when you die. There are many different types of annuities, so again, it is important to shop around.

 **LAWYER**

PROVIDING FOR THE FAMILY BUSINESS

If you are the sole proprietor of a business, then you need to give considerable thought to what will happen to that business in the event of your incapacity or death. Can the business continue to operate without you? Is it your intent that whoever inherits your business take over its daily operations or do you think it best to have the business sold and have the proceeds of the sale given to your beneficiary?

If you do not make provision for the orderly transfer of your business, then a court may need to make that decision for you. In particular, if you are declared incapacitated then your court appointed guardian will need court approval to continue the business. If you die, then the Personal Representative will decide whether to continue to operate the business (NCGS 28A-13-3(20)).

In addition to providing for continuation of the business operation, you need to consider how company debts will be paid. If your business is highly leveraged (business talk for "owes lots of money"), then you also need to consider how those loans will be paid, should you be unable to continue operating the business. We have already discussed key man insurance as a means of providing for funds to the company. An attorney who is experienced in business law (commercial law, corporation, banking, bankruptcy, franchise law, etc.) can offer other suggestions as to the best method of ensuring that the business continues its operation, or terminates in an orderly fashion — whichever is applicable in your case.

CHOOSING THE RIGHT ESTATE PLAN

Joint Ownership?
An In Trust For Account?
A Will?
A Revocable Living Trust?
An Insurance Policy???

This chapter offers so many options that the reader may be more confused than when he was blissfully unenlightened.

As with most things in life, you may find there are no ultimate solutions, just alternatives. The right choice for you is the one that best accomplishes your goal. This being the case, you first need to determine what you want to accomplish with the money that you leave. Think about what will happen to your property if you were to die suddenly, without making any plan different from the one you now have.

> Who will get your property?
> Will there be any estate tax?
> Will they need to go through probate?

If the answers to these questions are not what you wish, then you need to work to retitle your property to accomplish your goals. For those with significant assets, — especially those with estates large enough to pay estate taxes, a trip to an experienced Estate Planning attorney will be well worth the consultation fee.

YOUR ESTATE PLAN RECORD

Once you are satisfied with your estate plan, then the final thing to consider is whether your heirs will be able to locate your assets once you are deceased.

Most people have their business records in one place, their Will in another place, car titles and deeds in still another place. When someone dies, their beneficiaries may feel as if they are playing a game of "hide and seek" with the decedent. The game might be fun if it were not for the fact that things not found may be forever lost. For example, suppose you die in an accident and no one knows you are insured by your credit card company for accidental death in the amount of $25,000. The only one to profit is the insurance company, which is just that much richer because no one told them that you died as a result of an accident.

How about a key to a safe deposit box located in another state? Will anyone find it? Even if they find the key, how will they find the box?

It is not difficult to arrange things so that your affairs are always in order. It amounts to being aware of what you own (and owe) and keeping a record of your possessions. A side benefit is that by doing so, you will always know where all your business records are. If you ever spent time trying to collect information to file your taxes or trying to find a lost stock or bond certificate, you will appreciate the value of organizing your records.

Heirs need all the help they can get. It is difficult enough dealing with the loss, without the frustration of trying to locate important documents. Your heirs will have no problem locating your assets if you keep all of your records in a single place. It can be a desk drawer or a file cabinet or even a shoe box. It is helpful if you keep a separate file or folder for each type of investment. You might consider setting up the following folders:

📁 THE BANK & SECURITIES FOLDER

Store your original certificates for stocks, bonds, mutual funds, certificates of deposit, in a folder labeled BANK & SECURITIES FOLDER. In addition to the original certificate include a copy of the contract you signed with each financial institution. The contract will show where you have funds and who you named as beneficiary or joint owner of the account. If someone owes you money and has signed a promissory note or mortgage that identifies you as the lender, then you can store these documents in this folder as well.

If you wish to store your original documents in a safe deposit box, then keep a record of the location of the safe deposit box, and the number of the box, in this folder. Make a copy of all of the items stored in the box and place the copies in this folder. If you have an extra key to the box, then put the key in the folder. If you are the only person with access to the box, it may take a Probate procedure to remove items from the box once you die. Consider allowing someone you trust to be able to gain entry to the box in the event of your incapacity or death.

THE PERSONAL PROPERTY FOLDER

MOTOR VEHICLES

Put all motor vehicle titles in a Personal Property folder. This includes cars, mobile homes, boats, planes, etc. If you owe money on the vehicle, the lender may have possession of the original title certificate. If such is the case, then put a copy of the title certificate and registration in this folder. Put a copy of the promissory note or chattel mortgage in a separate liability folder.

If you have a boat or plane, then identify the location of the motor vehicle. For example, if you are leasing space in an airplane hanger or in a marina, keep a copy of the leasing agreement in this file.

JEWELRY

If you own expensive jewelry, keep a picture of the item together with the sales receipt or written appraisal in this folder.

COLLECTOR'S ITEMS

If you own a valuable art collection, or a coin collection or any other item of significant value, include a picture of the item in this file. Also include evidence of ownership of the item, such as a sales receipt or a certificate of authenticity, or a written appraisal of the item.

🗁 THE DEED FOLDER

Many people save every scrap of paper associated with the closing of real property. If you closed recently on real estate and there was a mortgage involved in the purchase, you probably walked away from closing with enough paper to wallpaper your kitchen. If you wish, you can keep all of those papers in a separate file that identifies the property, for example:

CLOSING PAPERS FOR THE CHARLOTTE PROPERTY.

Set aside the original deed (or a copy if the original is in a safe deposit box) and place it into a separate DEED FOLDER. Include deeds to parcels of real property, cemetery deeds, condominium deeds, cooperative shares to real property, timesharing certificates, etc. Include deeds to out of state property as well as North Carolina property in the DEED FOLDER. If you have a mortgage on your property, then put a copy of the mortgage and promissory note in a separate LIABILITY FOLDER.

🗁 THE INSURANCE/PENSION FOLDER

The INSURANCE FOLDER is for each original insurance policy that you own, be it car insurance, homeowner's insurance or a health care insurance policy. If you purchased real property, you probably received a title commitment at closing and the original title insurance policy some weeks later when you received your original deed from recording. If you cannot locate the title insurance policy, then contact the closing agent and have them send you a copy of your title policy. If you have a pension or an annuity, then include those documents in this folder as well.

📁 THE LIABILITY FOLDER

The LIABILITY FOLDER should contain all loan documents of debts that you owe. For example, if you purchased real property and have a mortgage on that property, then put a copy of the mortgage and promissory note in this folder. If you owe money on a car, put the promissory note and chattel mortgage on the car in the file. If you have a credit card, put a copy of the contract you signed with the credit card company in this file.

Many people never take the time to calculate their *net worth* (what a person owns less what that person owes). By having a record of your assets and outstanding debts, you can calculate your net worth whenever you wish.

📁 THE TAX RECORD FOLDER

Your Personal Representative (or next of kin) will need to file your final income tax returns. Keep a copy of your tax returns (both federal and state) for the past three years in your Tax Record Folder.

If you are a Federal Retiree, you should have received your **PERSONAL IDENTIFICATION NUMBER (PIN)** and the person who will inherit your pension (your *survivor annuitant*) should have received his/her own PIN as well. It is relatively simple to obtain this during your lifetime, but it may be difficult and/or stressful for your survivor annuitant to work through the system once you are gone. To get information on obtaining these numbers you can call the RETIREMENT INFORMATION OFFICE at (888) 767-6738. For the hearing impaired, call (800) 878-5707.

Upon your death, your survivor annuitant may be entitled to death benefits. These benefits are not paid automatically. Your survivor annuitant must apply for them by submitting a death claim to the Office of Personnel Management. Your survivor needs to know that it is necessary to apply and also how to apply. See page 32 for an explanation about how to apply for benefits and then make that information available to your family. You can either put this information in the insurance/pension folder or in your Personal Record folder.

THE PERSONAL RECORD FOLDER

The **PERSONAL RECORD FOLDER** should include documents that relate to you personally, such as a birth certificate, naturalization papers, pre-nuptial or post-nuptial agreement, Will or Trust Agreement, marriage certificate, divorce papers, army records, social security card; etc. If you have a Durable Power of Attorney for Health Care, or a Living Will, then this is a good place to keep those documents.

If you wish to keep a document in a safe deposit box, then keep a copy of the document in this folder and the original in the box.

In North Carolina, you have the right to deposit your original Will with the Clerk of the Superior Court. If you do so, then make a copy of the Will and leave a record of where the original is located.

THE *If I Die* FILE

In addition to keeping your up-to-date records in a single place, you need to let your family know the location of these items. You can set up an *If I Die* file and make that file accessible to someone you trust or to the person you appointed as Personal Representative in your Will; i.e., let that person know the location of the file and how to get it in the event of your death.

You can use the form on the next page as a basis for the information to include in the file.

If I Die

then the following information will help settle my estate:

INFORMATION FOR DEATH CERTIFICATE

MY FULL LEGAL NAME _____

MY SOCIAL SECURITY NO. _____

MY USUAL OCCUPATION _____

BIRTH DATE AND BIRTH PLACE _____

If naturalized, date & place _____

MY FATHER'S NAME _____

MY MOTHER'S MAIDEN NAME _____

PERSONS TO BE NOTIFIED OF MY DEATH

_____

_____

_____

FUNERAL AND BURIAL ARRANGEMENTS

LOCATION OF BURIAL SITE

_____

LOCATION OF PRENEED FUNERAL CONTRACT

_____

FOR VETERAN or SPOUSE BURIAL IN A NATIONAL CEMETERY

BRANCH_____SERIAL NO._____

VETERAN'S RANK _____

VETERAN'S VA CLAIM NUMBER _____

DATE AND PLACE OF ENTRY INTO SERVICE:

_____

DATE AND PLACE OF SEPARATION FROM SERVICE:

_____

LOCATION OF OFFICIAL MILITARY DISCHARGE
OR DD 214 FORM_____

LOCATION OF LEGAL DOCUMENTS

BIRTH CERTIFICATE _____

MARRIAGE CERTIFICATE_____

DIVORCE DECREE _____

PASSPORT _____

WILL OR TRUST _____

DEEDS _____

MORTGAGES _____

TITLE TO MOTOR VEHICLES _____

HEALTH CARE DIRECTIVES _____

NAME, PHONE NO. OF ATTORNEY_____

LOCATION OF FINANCIAL RECORDS

INSURANCE POLICIES:

NAME OF COMPANY & PHONE NO. _____

LOCATION OF POLICY _____

BENEFICIARY OF POLICY _____

PENSIONS/ANNUITIES:

IF FEDERAL RETIREE: PIN NUMBER: _____

NAME OF SURVIVOR _____

SURVIVOR PIN NUMBER _____

BANK

BANK: ACCOUNT NO._____

NAME, ADDRESS OF FINANCIAL INSTITUTION

_____

LOCATION OF SAFE DEPOSIT BOX _____

LOCATION OF KEY TO BOX _____

SECURITIES

NAME AND PHONE NUMBER OF BROKER

_____

TAX RECORDS FOR PAST 3 YEARS

LOCATION _____

WHEN TO UPDATE YOUR ESTATE PLAN

We discussed people's natural disinclination to make an estate plan until they are faced with their own mortality. Many believe that they will make just one Will and then die (maybe that's why they put off making a Will). The reality is, most people who make a Will change it at least once before they die.

If you have an estate plan, it is important to update it when any of the following events take place:

✍ RELOCATION TO A NEW STATE OR COUNTRY

If you move within state there is no need to change your estate plan, but if you move to another state or country, you need to check to see whether your plan is valid in that state. Each state (and country) has its own laws relating to the inheritance of property and those laws are very different from each other. Items that are protected from a creditor in one state, may not be creditor proof in another state. Each state has its own estate tax structure. If estate taxes are high, you may need an estate plan that will minimize the impact of those taxes.

Each state has its own, unique, laws of intestate succession. Who has the right to inherit your property in one state may be different from who can inherit your property in another. The rights of a spouse in a community property state are very different from those in other states. Even if you have a Will, what one state considers to be a valid Will, may be different from what another state considers to be valid. If you move to a another state or country, it is important to either educate yourself about the laws of the state, or to consult with an attorney who can assist you in reviewing your estate plan to see if that plan will accomplish your goals in that state.

If you move from the state and you have deposited your Will with the Clerk of the Superior Court, then you need to remember to get the original document back from the Clerk and take it with you to your new residence.

✍ A SIGNIFICANT CHANGE IN THE LAW

Once you have read this book, you will have the basic concept of the law, but laws change. It is important to keep up with those changes. You can do so by reading your daily newspaper, listening to the news on television and/or keeping in touch with your attorney to learn if any new law will affect your estate plan.

Tax laws are in a constant state of flux. You need to be aware of how the tax structure is being changed and how that change affects your estate plan. It is a good idea to discuss significant changes in the tax code with your accountant (or attorney) to learn how that change will affect you.

✍ A CHANGE IN RELATIONSHIP

If you get married, divorced, have a child, or a beneficiary of your estate dies, then you should examine your estate plan to determine whether it needs to be revised. If your marriage is annulled or you get divorced, there are certain changes that take place by law. For example, if you die without having changed your Will (or Trust), then any provision that you made for your ex-spouse in the Will or Trust will be read as if your ex-spouse died before you (NCGS 31-5.4). But it is important not to rely just on the law. Best to change all documents after the divorce. That includes Powers of Attorney For Health Care, deeds, Wills, etc. You should also change the beneficiary of your insurance policies, pension plans, etc.

GAMES DECEDENTS PLAY

We discussed the game of "hide and seek" some decedents play with their heirs. A variation of that game is the "wild goose chase." The person who plays this game is one who never updates his files. His records are filled with all sorts of lapsed insurance policies, promissory notes of debts long since paid; brokerage statements of securities that have been sold, and so on.

When he is gone, his familywill become frustrated as they vainly seek the "missing" asset.

If you wish to play this game, then the best joke is to keep the key to a safe deposit box that you are no longer leasing. That will keep folks hunting for a long time!

If you do not have a wicked sense of humor, then do your family a favor and update your records on a regular basis.

Completing The Process

The funeral is over.

Everyone went home.

You experienced and got past the initial grief.

All the affairs of the decedent have been settled.

But is the grieving over? Do you have closure? To use a tired expression, have you been able to "get on with your life" or do you find that you are still grieving?

And how about the children in the decedent's life?
How are they taking the loss?

The death event is not over until the family finally finds peace and acceptance of the loss. This book deals with issues that may arise as the family goes through the grieving process.

THE GRIEVING PROCESS

Psychologists have observed that it is common for a person to go through a series of stages as part of the grieving process. There is the initial shock of the death and often disbelief and denial:

"He can't be dead. I just spoke to him today!"

It is common for a mourner to be angry — angry at the decedent for dying — angry at a family member for something he should or shouldn't have done — just plain angry.

Sometimes an ill person is aware of his impending death and becomes angry, as if mourning his own death. Relations with the family may become strained under the stress of the illness. If there was an argument with the decedent, the bereaved may be left with an unresolved conflict and feelings of guilt.

Mourners often experience guilt. Many have an uneasy feeling that the death was somehow their fault. Some regret not having spent more time with the decedent. Others feel guilty because they weren't present when the decedent died.

There is grieving even when death is long expected and even welcomed. This was the case with a wife who nursed her husband at home for nine long years. Her husband suffered from debilitating strokes, a chronic heart condition, and finally failing kidneys. She often said "Some things are worse than death." When he died, she was shocked. He was close to death so many times. Each time he recovered. She couldn't believe he was dead. And she was surprised at the depth of her emotions. She thought she would be relieved. She didn't think she would experience such intense grief.

THE STAGES OF GRIEF

Although professionals in the fields of psychiatry and psychology have observed that guilt and anger are stages of grieving, there is no agreement about the number or composition of the stages of grieving. This is not surprising. The ways people react to death is as diverse as there are people. Some people seem not to grieve at all. Whether such people experience any stage of the mourning process may not be known even to the person himself/herself.

And there is diversity in grieving even in the same person. Each circumstance of death in one's life is different from another, so a person will grieve differently when different people in their life die. But for purposes of this discussion, we note that many people who lose someone they love report experiencing the following emotions and in the following sequence:

- initial shock, disbelief, alarm
- numbness, anger, guilt
- an intense longing for the deceased
- sadness, depression, loneliness
- recovery, acceptance of the loss, peace

Very often these emotions are accompanied by physical discomfort:

- tightness in chest, shoulders or throat
- over sensitivity to noise
- breathlessness, causing the person to sigh
- dry mouth
- muscular weakness
- loss of energy, fatigue

COPING WITH THE LOSS

How the general population deals with the death of a loved one was investigated in 1995 by the AMERICAN ASSOCIATION OF RETIRED PERSONS ("AARP"). AARP asked National Communications Research to conduct a telephone survey of over 5,000 people aged 40 or older. Approximately one third of the respondents reported that they had experienced the loss of a close friend or family member within the past year. Those reporting a loss were asked to describe specific coping activities that they had engaged in since the death of their loved one.

> 67% reported talking with friends and family
> 16% read an article or book about how to cope with death
> 9% received help with legal or practical arrangements
> 5% attended a grief support group

When asked what strategies they found to be most helpful in coping with their loss:

> 28% said talking with a friend or family member was most helpful
> 24% said their religion was most helpful
> 10% said knowing it was for the best
> 6% said memories of the deceased
> 4% reported staying busy as the best strategy.

It is interesting to note that 67% of the people who suffered a loss turned to family and friends to help them cope with the loss. Although talking with family and friends topped the list as the most commonly used strategy, only 28% reported this as being most helpful to them. Many times friends and family members want to help but they are at a loss as to what to say or do. The next section discusses different techniques that can be used to help with the grieving process.

HELPING THE BEREAVED

Family and friends want to help the person who is grieving, but sometimes they don't know how to do it. They may feel just as helpless in dealing with the loss as does the bereaved — not knowing what to say to console someone who is grieving.

There are no magic words, but saying you are sorry for the loss is appropriate and generally well received. Avoid platitudes such as: "It was fate." "It was God's will." "It was for the best." Especially avoid telling the bereaved that you know how he/she feels. People who suffer a great loss do not believe that anyone can understand how they feel; and they are probably correct. It is better to tell the bereaved what you are feeling:

"I was shocked when I heard of the death."
"I am so sad for you." "I am going to really miss him."

Knowing that you share the feeling of loss is comforting to someone who is grieving.

The wake or funeral is not the time express curiosity about how property is to be distributed. Statements such as "I gave that imported glass vase to your mother and I was wondering whether she remembered to tell you to give it to me" are at best tacky, if not downright insensitive.

Listening is more important than talking to the bereaved. They may need to explore the circumstances of the death — how the person died; where and when he died, etc. They may need to express what they are feeling, whether it be grief or anger. Try not to change the subject just because you are uncomfortable with the topic or with the expression of emotion. If the bereaved wishes to reminisce about the decedent, then join in the conversation. Talk about the decedent's good qualities and the enjoyable times that you shared together.

If during the funeral period, you want to do something such as prepare food or send flowers, then consider asking the bereaved for permission to do so. The family may prefer donations to a favorite charity in place of flowers. The family may have already made dinner plans for the guests. Do not make general offers of assistance. "Let me know if you need anything" is not likely to get a response even if the bereaved does need help with something. A better, more sincere approach, is a specific offer, such as, "If you need transportation, I can drive you to the cemetery."

Your assistance during the post-funeral period is more important than during the funeral period. During the funeral the bereaved is usually surrounded by family and friends and has more than ample assistance. Any offer to help at that time may not even register because the bereaved may be numb with grief — unable to comprehend what is going on around them — unable to even recall who was present at the funeral, nonetheless who offered assistance.

Once the funeral is over and everyone has gone home, that is the time to offer support. The bereaved needs to go through a transition period and must learn to live without the presence of their loved one. In general, the more dependent the bereaved was on the decedent, the more difficult the transition. In such case, you can be most helpful if you are able to offer assistance with those tasks of daily living that the bereaved is not accustomed to performing. For example, if the decedent was the sole driver in the family, you might help the bereaved to learn to drive or at least help find public transportation. If the decedent handled all of the family finances, you might assist the bereaved in bill paying and balancing a checkbook. If math is not your forte, help to find a bookkeeper who can assist for a reasonable fee.

But, the best thing that family and friends can do for the bereaved, is just to be there for them. As shown by the AARP survey, the specific coping activity used by the majority of the bereaved was to talk to a friend or relative. A telephone call, or a card, on a special anniversary or holiday will be appreciated. You can help most with a call or a visit. It is just that simple.

Also be patient with the bereaved. There is no set time to get through the grieving process. It may take considerable time for the mourner to be able to find some quality of life. If several months have passed and you are concerned that the bereaved is still not functioning well, or at least better, then you might consider suggesting that the bereaved seek professional counseling. Try not to be judgmental when making the suggestion. Don't say "You should be feeling better by now," but rather, "I can see that you are still having a hard time getting through this difficult period. Have you considered seeing _____?"

Suggest whatever is appropriate to the mourner. For example, if the mourner is a religious person, suggest a visit with his/her religious leader. If the mourner is a social person, suggest a support group. If the bereaved is severely depressed, then a visit to a doctor or psychiatrist may be the best recommendation.

Do not expect your recommendation to be well received. The mourner may become angry or annoyed that you even made the suggestion. It may be difficult for the mourner to accept the fact that he/she needs assistance. Some people, mostly men, think it an admission of weakness to agree that they need help. They believe they should be able to "tough it out."

Some mourners may have increased their consumption of alcohol or turned to drugs in an attempt to deal with the pain that they are experiencing. If they accept your suggestion, they may need to deal with a growing addiction, in addition to the problem of overcoming the grief, and they may not be willing to do that.

Elderly people might think there is a stigma associated with any kind of counseling. They may insist "There's nothing wrong with me" fearing that you think they are unbalanced or somehow mentally defective.

Some people, especially the overachiever type, refuse to seek counseling because they perceive asking for help to be a sign of failure — an admission that they failed to work out the problem themselves. It's as if they failed "Grieving 101."

But those most resistant to a suggestion of a need for counseling are mourners who use denial as a defense mechanism. They may brush off the suggestion with "No. I'm alright" or "I'm doing a lot better." People who deny that they are having trouble getting past the grief, do not want to deal with the problem. If they deny that they have a problem, then they don't have a problem and that solves that!

In such cases, the timeworn adage, "You can lead a horse to water, but you can't make him drink," applies. The mourner needs to take the first step himself. You cannot take it for him. All you can do is assure the mourner (and yourself) that you have confidence that he/she can, and will, work this through.

HELPING A CHILD THROUGH THE LOSS

The first thing parents observe about their second child is how very different that child is from their first child. Parents quickly learn that each of their children is an individual, with his/her own separate response to any given situation. It is important to keep this fact in mind when trying to assist a child through the loss of a close family member or friend. Because each child is different, there is no single proper way to assist a child through a period of mourning. You can help the child most if you consider the child's background as it relates to the loss:

What is the child's relationship to the decedent?
What were the circumstances of the death?
Was it expected or was it sudden or tragic?
What is the emotional age of the child? That age may differ significantly from his/her chronological age.

As an example, consider the family of Harold and Elaine, parents of three children. Emily, the eldest child, was one of those "born old" children, wise beyond her years, sensitive and shy. Her brother John, two years her junior was the direct opposite — boisterous, immature, constantly in motion. Peter came along five years later. He was the baby of the family, a cherub, always smiling, indulged by parents and siblings.

When their paternal grandfather died, Emily was 10, John, 8 and Peter, 3. Their parents expected the death because "Gramps" had been suffering from cancer for a long time. No mention was made to the children of the serious nature of the illness, so Emily was surprised to learn of the death. She shed no tears but retreated to her room and soon became occupied with a computer game.

John and his father cried together when they were told that Gramps had died. Gramps was both kind and generous with a great sense of humor. Best of all he was never critical of John's rambunctious behavior. John and his Dad felt that they lost the best friend they ever had.

Peter did not understand what was going on; but he reacted empathetically, patting John on the shoulder, and saying "Don't cry Johnny."

When it came time to go to the funeral Emily refused to go. Johnny got angry with Emily for something or another and pushed her down. She was not hurt, but she cried loudly and carried on. Peter started whining. The whole day was hard on their parents.

The next few months were equally difficult. John woke up with nightmares. Emily was sullen and withdrawn. No one mentioned the death except Peter who was full of questions: "Where's Gramps?"
"Was he in that box?"
"Where did they put the box?"
"Why was everyone crying?"

Harold and Elaine were having their own problems dealing with the loss and they had no patience with the children. The family eventually got back to normal, but it might have been easier on all of them had the parents prepared the children for the dying process.

PREPARING FOR THE EVENT

Most deaths are expected. The majority of people who die are ill for several months before their death. Children are not always aware of a family member's mortal illness so it may come as a shock to them when it happens. It might have been easier on Emily and John if their parents said something like:

> *Gramps is old and very ill. It happens that all living*
> *things, plants, animals and people, eventually die.*
> *No one knows for sure when someone will die, but*
> *it may be that because he is so old and so very sick*
> *that Gramps may die sometime within the year.*

If either child wanted to pursue the subject, then that could lead to a discussion of the funeral process:

> *When someone dies in our family, all of our friends*
> *and family gather together to talk about how much*
> *we loved the person and how much we will miss*
> *having that person with us. Later we go to the*
> *gravesite where we say prayers and our last good-byes.*

It is important for parents to explain the children's role in this process, but like most couples, Harold and Elaine never thought about, much less discussed, their children's participation in the funeral and burial service. Had her parents told Emily what to expect and what was expected of her, she might not have objected to attending the funeral.

Before discussing the matter with the child, it is important that a husband and wife explore their own views on their children's participation in a funeral and burial. They may find that they have differing views on the following issues:

What factors should determine whether a child attends the wake and/or funeral:
  ▷ custom or convenience?
  ▷ the age and emotional maturity of that child?
  ▷ the relationship of the child to the decedent?

Should the child be allowed to decide whether he/she wishes to attend the wake and/or funeral?

Should a child be allowed (or encouraged) to touch or kiss the corpse?

Should children participate in grave site ceremonies?

Should a child be encouraged or required to visit the grave site at a later date?

There are no right or wrong answers for any of the above questions. Each family has its own set of customs and values and the answers to these questions need to conform to those customs and values. What is important is that the couple agree about what they expect of their children and then impart that expectation to their children.

The "imparting" is the difficult part. No one likes to talk about death. Parents have been told that they need to discuss sex with their children. They have been told that they need to discuss drugs with their children. These are important, life threatening, issues but it is entirely possible that a child will grow to be an adult without ever having someone close to them die. So why bring up the subject?

The reason to discuss the matter is the same reason to discuss sex with your children. The sex they see on television or hear about from their friends is a reflection of societal values but perhaps not your family values. You discuss sex to impart your family values and expectations to your children. If you wish to express to your children your views on the dying process and the afterlife (or the lack of it, if that is your belief) then it is appropriate to discuss these matters when you believe the child is sufficiently mature and ready for the discussion.

Still another reason to discuss death with the child is when someone close to them is quite aged or seriously ill. If they heard that some family member is dying, they may have concerns or questions that you can answer. Most children fear the unknown and death is an unknown to them. Of course, children are aware of the fact of death almost as soon as they can speak. It is all around them. Animated characters "die" as part of a computer game. Children's cartoon movies and television shows contain death and dying scenes. A child may have a pet that dies. Children hear about people dying almost nightly on the news.

Although children are familiar with the concept of death, they do not know how they or their family will react to the death of a loved one. If the topic is discussed prior to an impending death, the child may find it comforting to know what to expect, what behavior is expected of them, and what choices they may have regarding their attendance at a wake or funeral.

AFTER THE FUNERAL

Once the funeral is over, you need to deal with your own loss. That may be a difficult process for you so you may not even notice that your child is also grieving. This was the case with Harold and Elaine. They were not aware that Emily was having a difficult time with the loss — after all she didn't even cry when she heard of the death. If they thought about it, they may have realized that Emily was retreating into herself as a defense mechanism for dealing with the loss. Her continued sullen attitude after the funeral was a tip off that she was having difficulty getting beyond the loss.

If her parents encouraged Emily to talk about the problem, they would have learned that she had ambivalent feelings about her grandfather. She loved him, but she felt that he favored her brothers. Gramps always played "boy" games of catch and touch football. For her, there was none of the camaraderie that John enjoyed. Gramps never took the time to get to know Emily and she resented that. Now that he was gone, there would be no opportunity for her to have a meaningful relationship with her grandfather.

People are helped most by talking with a friend or relative about their loss. The same applies to children. Emily could have profited had she been able to explore her feelings with either of her parents. Her parents might also have profited because they may have developed a closer relationship with Emily and established a pattern of open communication.

As it was, Emily never did resolve the problem. Her parents suffered her sullenness without ever a clue as to what Emily was all about. Unfortunately, this lack of communication continued as Emily grew older and ever more a closed book.

John fared better. Harold recognized that John's nightmares were related to the loss. Harold made an effort to spend more time with the boy and not to be so critical when John acted up.

As for Peter, his parents tried to answer his questions as best as they were able. Elaine had the uneasy feeling that she was not answering them "the right way." She thought she made a mistake by saying that "Gramps is now at rest" because Peter asked if Gramps was sleeping. She thought that she might have caused Peter to confuse death and sleep.

Had Elaine investigated she could have found any number of excellent publications dealing with the subject. Many funeral homes provide families with complimentary pamphlets on how to answer children's questions about death. The local library and bookstore have any number of excellent publications designed to answer questions raised by small children.

Most religious organizations offer printed material for young people that explain death from the organization's perspective. For religious families, this is a good opportunity for the family to discuss their religious beliefs as they relate to the loss of a loved one.

INTERNET RESOURCES

Many Web sites offer free publications on how to deal with the issues of death and dying. Today's child is computer literate. A child may, on his own, decide to seek an E-mail buddy to work through a problem the child may be having with the death. Parents need to supervise such communication because the child may be especially vulnerable at this point in his/her life.

✂✂✂✂✂✂✂✂✂✂✂✂✂✂✂✂✂✂✂✂✂✂✂✂✂✂✂✂✂

GriefNet   **(734) 761-1960**
P.O. Box 3272
Ann Arbor, MI 48106-3272

GriefNet offers E-mail grief support groups. This Web site is operated by Rivendell Resources, a non-profit organization. KIDSAID is a companion Web site to GriefNet. They offer peer support groups for children who are dealing with a loss. Parental permission is required before the child can join a support group.
   http://www.griefnet.org/KIDSAID/kidstokids.htm
       E-mail: visibility@griefnet.org

✂✂✂✂✂✂✂✂✂✂✂✂✂✂✂✂✂✂✂✂✂✂✂✂✂✂✂✂✂

TAG: Teen Age Grief, Inc.   (661) 253-1932
P.O. Box 220034
Newhall, CA 91322-0034

Teen Age Grief, Inc. is a non-profit organization. Their primary function is to provide expertise in grief support to grieving teens.
       http://www.smartlink.net/~tag/
       E-mail: tag@smartlink.net

THE TROUBLED CHILD

Most deaths are from natural causes. The death is expected and not all that difficult for the family to finally accept. The ***problem death*** is one that is tragic, unexpected, and/or a death that cuts short a life. More and more school officials are recognizing that the loss of a member of the school community deeply affects the student population. Many schools have adopted a policy of having school psychologists counsel the students as soon as the death occurs. They do not wait until a school child shows signs of being disturbed by the event.

It would be well for parents to adopt the same policy. Specifically, if your family suffers a problem death then consider seeking the services of a professional who is experienced in grief counseling just as soon after the death as is practicable. The next day is none too soon.

A case in point was that of a 14 year old girl who lived with her grandmother, a jovial, robust woman whose main pleasures in life were eating and telling funny stories. One morning when they were eating their usual breakfast of fried eggs, sausage and buttered toast, the grandmother complained about her doctor and how her doctor was on her case about losing weight and lowering her cholesterol. She no sooner finished the sentence when she suffered a heart attack. She died within minutes.

This was a problem death. The death was both unexpected and tragic. Unexpected because the grandmother looked quite healthy. Tragic, because it occurred in the presence of the granddaughter.

No one knew how deeply this affected the girl until a few months had passed. The girl was losing quite a bit of weight. When questioned, she said that it was over-eating that caused her grandmother's death and she wanted to be sure that she ate a healthy diet with absolutely no fat. Concerned family members explained that losing too much weight was just as bad as being overweight. The girl agreed with them, but she continued to lose weight.

When family members realized the severity of the problem they took her to a doctor, who in turn referred them to a psychiatrist. The diagnosis was anorexia. Unfortunately, no amount of therapy, antidepressant, or medical intervention helped. The girl died a year later.

A death does not always need to be a problem death to cause a problem for a child. If a child has unresolved issues with the decedent, then that child may need professional assistance in coping with the loss. Children do not manifest grief or depression in the same way as adults, so look for changes that are atypical of the child and that do not resolve themselves within a reasonable time after the death. Consider consulting with a child psychologist if your child exhibits unusual or antisocial behavior such as:

> eating too much or too little

> destructive or aggressive behavior

> sleeping too much or too little

> misbehaving at school

> a sudden change in school performance

The red flag, signaling an immediate need for counseling, is a child who talks or writes about committing suicide. It is important to act quickly to show the child that you understand that he/she is having a rough time and that you and the doctor want to help the child get through this difficult period.

There are any number of resources in the community to assist the child, from school counselors to religious organizations. The North Carolina Psychological Association, located in Raleigh, can refer you to psychologists in your county who are experienced in grief counseling. Their telephone number is (919)872-1005.

For those who cannot afford private care, counties offer low-cost services on an ability to pay basis. Some religious organizations offer counseling services to their members, as well as to the general public, on a sliding scale basis.

Before seeking counseling services, it is important to schedule a physical checkup for the child. There is a chance that the problem is physiological. Some illnesses cause behavioral changes; for example, food allergies can cause aggressive behavior. Hearing or visual deficiencies can cause a child to withdraw into himself. Even infections can cause behavioral disturbances. Perhaps the child is on drugs and an examination should pick that up. All these things need to be ruled out prior to counseling.

If your child has been treated by the physician over the years, the doctor may know the child well enough to be able to offer some insight into the problem. If the examination does not reveal a physical problem, the physician may be able to suggest the right type of treatment, i.e., psychologist or psychiatrist, and perhaps give you a referral.

CHOOSING THE RIGHT COUNSELOR

There was a film called GOOD WILL HUNTING in which a brilliant, but troubled, teenager was required, by court order, to attend counseling. The funniest part of the film was the manner in which the boy went through counselors. He deliberately alienated (and was alienated) by many doctors until he met the right one for him. Similarly, if your child needs counseling you may need to interview several counselors before you find someone with whom your child can work; someone who speaks on his/her level — someone the child can trust.

The issue of trust may create a dilemma for the parent. The child is the counselor's patient. The counselor cannot betray the child's trust by revealing what was said during treatment, yet parents need to know whether the treatment is helping the child. The counselor can, and should, disclose to the parent the diagnosis, prognosis and type of proposed treatment. The parents need to employ someone they trust to pursue the course of treatment that they determine is best for their child.

In seeking a counselor, personal references are the best avenue. With or without references, you need to investigate the counselor's background. What is his/her training? What percentage of the practice is devoted to grief counseling children in this age group? Interview more than one counselor before making your choice. If the child is sufficiently mature and able to cooperate in choosing the right counselor, then that is an important step forward. If not, you may need to be assertive and go with the counselor with whom you are most comfortable. If it turns out that there is no improvement within a few months, then you need to find another counselor. As with the student in GOOD WILL HUNTING, it may take several tries before you come upon someone who can help your child.

THE ADULT ORPHAN

The baby boomers are a unique group in many ways. What other group has transition periods marked by headlines? "Baby Boomers Turn 50" is the latest newsworthy event. The "Adult Orphan" is a condition unique to that age group. Most Boomers have had their parents with them for half a century. Their parents have survived longer than any other generation in recorded history. But now the Boomers' parents are in their 80s and 90s and Boomers will need to learn to live without them.

Many have functioned independently for years and can handle the loss without problem. For others it is overwhelming. That was the case with two sisters. Opposites from birth. Patti was an independent spirit. Rebellious, strong-willed, she left her hometown to go to college and never looked back. She didn't even resemble her sister Maria. Maria was short, dark-haired, with a bit of a weight problem. Patti looked like an aging flower child with long, straight hair. You'd hardly pick them out as sisters, except for the fact of the resemblance to their parents. Patti had her Dad's angular features (especially his sharp nose), and Maria, her mother's round face and large dark eyes.

Maria lived within 10 miles of her parents all her life. It was a great shock when her Dad died suddenly of a heart attack. But her mother was there to comfort her and offer her words of encouragement, even though her Mom was struggling with the loss herself. That was the way Mom was. Always putting the needs of her children before her own. Patti was the strong one at Dad's funeral. Making funeral arrangements. Greeting family members. Helping Mom to settle Dad's estate. She seemed to know exactly what needed to be done and how to do it.

Maria seemed as dependent as Patti was independent. Maybe it was Maria's personality. Maybe she was raised that way. Maybe her parents needed Maria to need them as much as Maria needed to lean on them.

"Co-dependent" taunted Patti.

How Maria hated that phrase!

Maria never thought of herself as being dependent. She married and raised two children of her own. Over the last few years she took care of her mother as her mother's health failed. Maria's whole day revolved around her mother. Making sure she was fed and comfortable. Maria did not know what she would do with all her time now that her role of caretaker was done. But the emotional loss was the hardest part. Her mother had been her closest confident, her best friend.

Maria held up better at the funeral than she had expected. It was Patti who seemed to fall apart. When Maria thought about it she understood. Her parents gave Patti unconditional love. Patti found that nowhere else. All other relationships in her life were flawed. Her two marriages ended in divorce and that bothered her greatly. Bad enough to make a mistake once. How could she have been so stupid as to pick two losers? Yet her parents neither condemned nor criticized. They were there for Patti emotionally and financially. They were her safety net. Now they were both gone.

At the funeral Maria looked over at Patti. She seemed lost, like a motherless child, an orphan. Now Patti would need to grow old without her parents. Now she would need to grow up.

STRATEGIES TO COPE WITH THE LOSS

Once a person accepts the fact of death, they are past the initial phase of the grief process. Most people do very well and are able to go through the remaining stages with no overt effort on their part. Others suffer profoundly and need to find ways to get through the grieving process. If you have recently experienced a loss and are having difficulty coping with the loss then consider your own personality type and explore those strategies that might help you through.

Do you enjoy socializing with people or do you prefer solitary activities? Are you a "do-it-yourself" type of person or do you feel more at ease with someone leading you through the process?

STRATEGIES FOR THE PRIVATE PERSON

If you find socializing to be difficult, consider non-social activities such as reading a self help book. There are many excellent publications that explore the grieving process and how to adjust to the loss. Praying or quiet meditation may offer you consolation. This may be a good time to explore different kinds of meditative techniques. You can find books on meditative techniques such as Zen or visualization in the Philosophy section of the library or bookstore. You can find books on Yoga in the exercise section.

If you are computer literate, you can use your browser to locate an Internet support group. An anonymous friend may be the perfect confidant to help you to work through the sadness and loneliness that you are feeling. You can locate E-mail support groups for people who are dealing with all types of grief issues by searching the following topics: GRIEF   MOURNING   DEATH   DYING

STRATEGIES FOR THE SOCIAL MINDED

If you are a social person, consider using those types of activities that involve a social setting, such as joining a bridge club, or a bowling or golfing group. If your grief is too deep to concentrate on recreational activities, consider joining a support group. The power of the support group is companionship. They offer the one thing you may need most at this time — just someone to listen.

If you belong to an organized religion or a civic organization, find out whether they have a support group for people who are going through the grieving process. If your organization does not have a support group, then consider starting one yourself. It can be as simple as putting a notice in a weekly bulletin that you are holding a meeting for anyone who lost a loved one within the past year. You can hold the meeting as part of a picnic or barbecue with everyone bringing a dish for others to share. Just getting together and sharing experiences may help you and others in your organization as well.

If you do not belong to an organization, then look in the newspaper for notices of meetings of local support groups or consider joining one of the many national support groups. The following are some of the well established national groups:

FOR WIDOWED PERSONS

THEOS   (412) 471-7779
(They Help Each Other Spiritually)
322 Boulevard of the Allies, Suite 105
Pittsburgh, PA 15222-1919

THEOS is a national organization with a volunteer network of recently widowed persons. They have support chapters in many states. If you wish to establish a support group in your area, they will help you to do so.

🕊🕊🕊🕊🕊🕊🕊🕊🕊🕊🕊🕊🕊🕊🕊🕊🕊🕊🕊🕊🕊🕊🕊🕊🕊🕊🕊🕊🕊🕊🕊🕊🕊

AARP GRIEF AND LOSS PROGRAM
WIDOWED PERSONS SERVICE   (800) 424-3410
601 E Street NW
Washington, DC 20049

AARP has support groups for widowed persons throughout the United States. They also have support groups for adults who have suffered the loss of a family member such as a parent or sibling. You can call the above 800 number and they will let you know if there is a support group in your area.

E-mail: griefandloss@ aarp.org
Web site: www.aarp.org/griefprograms

FOR WIDOWED PARENTS

PARENTS WITHOUT PARTNERS (800)637-7974
401 N. Michigan Avenue
Chicago, IL 60611-6267

PARENTS WITHOUT PARTNERS is a national non-profit organization for single parents. They offer group discussions and single parent activities such as picnics and hikes. Their national headquarters in Illinois can direct you to the chapter nearest you.

PARENTS WITHOUT PARTNERS WEB SITE
http://parentswithoutpartners.org
E-mail: pwp@sba.com

PET GRIEF SUPPORT SERVICES

Those who suffer the loss of a pet may experience a sense of loss similar to the loss of a close family member. Often they hesitate to turn to friends or family members (especially those who never owned a pet) believing they just wouldn't understand.

Some local Humane Societies provide a pet loss counseling service. Some veterinarian medical schools have volunteer counseling services.

There is a list of pet grief counseling
services for other states at
http://www.superdog.com/

THE PHYSICAL ASPECTS OF GRIEVING

As discussed, accompanying the emotional stages of grief, are physical symptoms that mourners commonly experience, such as tightness in the chest; muscular weakness; loss of energy and fatigue.

It is just as important to deal with the physical aspects of grieving as it is with the emotional. People who suffer extreme grief tend to become extreme in everyday activities. They may forget to eat. Some find themselves eating all day. Some mourners develop sleep disturbances and go without sleep for long periods of time while others suffer the opposite extreme of wanting to sleep all day. If you find that your grief is affecting your physical wellbeing, you need to make a conscious effort to care for yourself:

☆ EAT A BALANCED NUTRITIONAL DIET

Contrary to popular taste, sugar, salt, fat and chocolate do not constitute the four basic food groups. And contrary to current food faddism, no one diet fits all. The ability to digest certain foods varies from person to person and we all have ethnic preferences. You need to learn what balance of fats, protein (meat, fish, legumes) and carbohydrates (fruit, vegetables, grains) you require to maintain your optimum weight and state of well being; and then make an effort to keep that balance in your daily diet.

☆ GET SUFFICIENT REST

There is much variation in the amount of sleep required from person to person. You know how much sleep you normally require. Try to maintain your usual, pre-loss, sleep pattern. If you are finding difficulty sleeping at night, resist the urge to sleep during the day. It is easy to reverse your days and nights. Awake all night, dozing all day, will only make you feel as if you are walking around in a fog.

☆ EXERCISE EACH DAY

Exercise can be as simple as taking a brisk 20 minute walk, however the more sustained and energetic, the greater the benefit. If you are having trouble sleeping at night, try exercising during the late afternoon and eating your main meal at lunch rather than late at night.

Eating right, getting sufficient sleep, exercising — most people have heard these recommendations from so many sources (doctors, psychologists, writers for health magazines, etc.) that they seem to have become a cliche. But the reason that so many professionals make these suggestions is simply that they work. Doing all these things should make you feel significantly better.

And this may be the time for a complete physical checkup. Grieving is hard on the body. The cause of your physical discomfort may not emotional. It could be that there is a medical problem that needs attending.

ADJUSTING TO A NEW LIFE STYLE

If you lost a member of your immediate family, then in addition to going through the stages of the grieving process, you need to go through a transition period in which you learn how to live without the decedent. The child must learn to live without the guidance of a parent. Parents may need to put their parenting behind them. The spouse must learn to live without a partner, and as a single person.

In addition to learning to live with the loss, the bereaved may need to establish a new identity. Such was the case with Claire. She and Fred were married 44 years when he died after a lengthy battle with cancer. At first Claire didn't think she could live without him. She had been a wife for so long. She had trouble thinking of herself as a single person — nonetheless being one.

Claire had difficulty accepting the fact that Fred was dead, even though she expected he would die for months before he did. She would see Fred in her dreams. Sometimes she thought she saw him sitting in his favorite chair. When Fred appeared to Claire, he looked the same as when they were first married. Sometimes she thought he was speaking to her.

What was most comforting to Claire was that Fred was smiling at her. She was relieved to know that Fred was no longer in pain and was at peace. The smile on his face was a relief to her because she feared he might be angry with her for the many times he would call out her name and she would become annoyed with him. She felt guilty that she did not have more patience as a caregiver.

Claire found herself talking to Fred especially during those times that she was undecided as to what to do. As time progressed, she began to incorporate her husband's beliefs into her own so that instead of asking herself "What should I do?" it became "This is what Fred would have done."

Eventually Claire found that she was able to function on her own. She began to re-engage with the world. She found new interests to pleasantly occupy her time. She learned how to live as a single person. She is now more self sufficient than at any other time in her life. She laments that Fred no longer visits her. She still misses him.

Claire was able to get beyond the grief. She did it on her own, though she will tell you that she did it with Fred's help.

Claire's case is not unusual. As verified by the AARP survey, most people adjust to the loss on their own, requiring only an assist from family and friends, but there is a percentage of the grieving population that will require assistance and need to seek professional grief counseling.

For those experiencing psychological problems prior to the death, the event of the death may be the precipitating factor to mental illness requiring treatment. Similarly, if a person had a drinking problem or a drug addiction before the death, the event of the death may exacerbate the addiction.

Some deaths are so violent or tragic, that even the sturdiest may be unable to resume their life without professional assistance. In the next section, we discuss ways of coping with the problem death.

THE PROBLEM DEATH

As discussed, the problem death is one that is unexpected, tragic or a death that cuts short a life. Such a death is an immediate problem in terms of the funeral, burial and estate settlement, but the most difficult problem is getting through the mourning period.

The death of a child is always a problem death. Even if the child is an adult, the parent experiences extreme grief. No one expects to outlive his or her child. In these days of a lengthening life cycle, more and more parents may come to experience such a loss. The loss may come at a time when the parent is frail or in poor health, making it all the more difficult to deal with the loss.

The only thing harder than losing an adult child is losing a young child. Nothing compares to the intensity of grief experienced by a parent when a little one dies. Some parents believe they are losing their mind. Many feel that their lives can never have meaning again. Guilt and recrimination flow, "Maybe I could have prevented it." There is even guilt for returning to ordinary living. If the parents find themselves smiling, laughing or making love they think, "How can we be doing this? How can we ever be normal again?"

The family who experiences a tragic or violent death should consider seeking professional grief counseling as soon as practicable after the death. The grief counseling can be in the format of a self-help group. Participants are able to talk and share their pain with others like themselves who understand what they are experiencing.

There are many specialized self-help groups that provide literature and peer support for families who experience a problem death.

FOR PRENATAL OR NEONATAL DEATHS

M.E.N.D. **M**ommies **E**nduring **N**eonatal **D**eath
P.O. Box 1007   (888)-695-MEND
Coppell, TX   75019

MEND provides monthly newsletters and has a Web site that provides information:.

http://www.mend.org
E-mail rebekah@mend.org

🐾🐾🐾🐾🐾🐾🐾🐾🐾🐾🐾🐾🐾🐾🐾🐾🐾🐾🐾🐾🐾🐾🐾🐾🐾🐾🐾🐾🐾🐾🐾

SHARE   (800) 821-6819
National Share Pregnancy and Infant Loss Support
St. Joseph Health Center
300 First Capitol Drive
St. Charles, MO   63301-2893

SHARE is a resource center for bereaved parents. They have support groups throughout the United States. You can call the national office for the telephone number of the support group in your state.

http://www.nationalshareoffice.com
E-mail share@nationalshareoffice.com

FOR FAMILIES OF A DECEASED CHILD

THE COMPASSIONATE FRIENDS
National Chapter: (630) 990-0010
P.O. Box 3696, Oak Brook, IL 60522
THE COMPASSIONATE FRIENDS have local chapters with
volunteers (themselves bereaved parents) to accept
telephone calls.

http://www.compassionatefriends.org
E-mail   tcf_national@prodigy.com

꙰꙰꙰꙰꙰꙰꙰꙰꙰꙰꙰꙰꙰꙰꙰꙰꙰꙰꙰꙰꙰꙰꙰꙰꙰꙰꙰꙰꙰꙰꙰꙰꙰꙰꙰

A.G.A.S.T   (888) 774-7437
ALLIANCE OF GRANDPARENTS A SUPPORT IN TRAGEDY
P.O. Box 17281
Phoenix, AZ 85011-0281
AGAST supports grandparents, who have suffered the
loss of a grandchild, with informational packets,
peer contact and newsletters.

E-mail: GRANMASIDS@AOL.COM

꙰꙰꙰꙰꙰꙰꙰꙰꙰꙰꙰꙰꙰꙰꙰꙰꙰꙰꙰꙰꙰꙰꙰꙰꙰꙰꙰꙰꙰꙰꙰꙰꙰꙰꙰

SIDS ALLIANCE   (800) 221-7437
SUDDEN INFANT DEATH SYNDROME ALLIANCE
1314 Bedford Avenue, Suite 210
Baltimore, MD 21208

The SIDS Alliance is a national, not-for-profit,
voluntary organization. Their Web site offers
information and the names and E-mail addresses of
chapters in all of the states.

http//www.sidsalliance.org
E-mail: sids@ais.net

FOR FAMILIES OF MURDERED CHILDREN

THE NATIONAL ORGANIZATION OF   (888) 818-POMC
PARENTS **O**F **M**URDERED **C**HILDREN, INC.
National Chapter
100 East Eighth Street, B-41
Cincinnati, OH   45202

POMC has support groups and contact people in each of the fifty states. You can contact the National Chapter for the group nearest you.

http://www.pomc.com
E-mail natlpomc@aol.com

FOR FAMILIES OF SUICIDES

AMERICAN ASSOC. OF SUICIDOLOGY   (202) 237-2280
4201 Connecticut Ave. NW, Suite 408
Washington, DC 20008

The American Association of Suicidology is a not-for-profit organization that promotes education, public awareness and research for suicide prevention. It serves as a national clearinghouse for information on suicide. You can call for the number of a support group nearest you. Their Web site has the names addresses and phone number of several organizations that offer counseling for families who have lost a loved one to suicide.

http://www.suicidology.org

BUT WHAT IF I CAN'T STOP GRIEVING?

We observed that there are five stages of grieving:
shock/disbelief
anger/guilt
searching/pining
sadness/depression
acceptance of the loss.

There is no right way to grieve. You may pass through a stage rapidly or even skip a stage. You may get hung up in one of the stages and have difficulty getting beyond that emotion. Some psychologists refer to this as "stuckness." It's something like what happened to 45-rpm phonograph records that were popular in the 1940's and 1950's.

For the benefit of the digital generation who have no experience with phonographs, the record was played by means of a needle that glided over groves of a revolving disk (the record). Sometimes the needle would get stuck in a groove and play the same sound over and over again until the annoyed listener bumped it into the next groove.

If you are stuck in one of the stages of mourning, you may think the suggestions in this section to be useless in your situation because they encourage you to be proactive, i.e., to actively seek to help yourself. If you are thinking:
"I **can't** help myself. " or
"If I could help myself, I wouldn't have this problem," then the first thing you need to understand, and accept, is that you have no other choice but to help yourself. The pain exists within you and nowhere else. Because the pain is internal and unique to you, only you can ease that pain. This does not mean that no one can help you to deal with the pain. It just means that you need to be interactive with the healing process; and in particular, you need to take the first step.

What is that first step? To answer that question you need to identify those areas of your life with which you are having difficulty. It might help to make a list of all of the things that are bothering you. Once you compose the list, look at the last item on the list. If you are like most people, you will initially avoid thinking about what is really troubling you. It may take the last item on the list for you to admit to yourself what is really causing the problem.

Once you identify the problem, the identification itself should suggest the solution. For example, suppose you find the holidays unbearable, then a solution may be to change your holiday routine. Instead of wearing yourself out shopping for gifts, use the money to treat yourself to a boat cruise. Tell everyone that this year you are taking a holiday from the holidays. You may find that people are just as tired of exchanging gifts as you are and that they gladly welcome the change.

If your problem is being lonely, then your solution will involve companionship. How you find companionship depends on your personality. If you are lonely, but not a social person, consider adopting a pet. If you are civic minded, you may find companionship as a volunteer for community activities. If you are physically active, perhaps you can take up a new sport or even pick up a sport that you used to enjoy at an earlier time in your life. If you enjoy sports but are not in the best shape, perhaps you can coach children's team sports.

If your problem is that you are severely depressed, the solution will involve medical and/or psychological methods of lifting the depression. If you decide to ask for medical assistance, you need to continue to be interactive. You cannot stand passively by saying "Now heal me." Pharmaceutical hyperbole notwithstanding, there is no magic pill. An antidepressant may help you to gain control of yourself, but you still need to work through the grief.

Make an effort to concentrate on things in your life that are right, as opposed to thoughts that make you angry or sad. This may be difficult to do. During periods of high stress, you may feel as if your mind has a mind of its own. Thoughts may race through your mind even though you'd just as soon not think them. Prayer and/or meditation may help you to reestablish discipline in your thinking process.

If you feel that you have tried it all and you still are unable to find peace and contentment in your life, then you need to ask the hard question:

"What is it about mourning that I really enjoy?"

Strange question?
Not really.

You may enjoy thinking of your loved one even if the thought gives you as much pain as pleasure. You may think that if you stop mourning then you truly lose the decedent. If that's the case, then compartmentalize your grief, that is, set aside a special time of the day to actively think about and/or grieve for your loved one and the rest of the day not to grieve or even think about the decedent.

Actively plan the grieving compartment of your day. You may wish to have a grieving routine, perhaps visit the grave site once a week; or quietly spend 15 minutes a day looking at pictures of the decedent or writing down your memories of the happy times you had together. If you have been discussing your grief with family or friends, restrict such talks to specific times, perhaps on the decedent's birthday, or on the anniversary of his death.

Set aside as much time each day as you believe you need to mourn, but here is the hard part — you need to exercise self restraint not to mourn, nor talk about, nor even think of the decedent during any other part of the day. If your mind wanders back to the sadness and loneliness of the loss, postpone it. Say to yourself, "Hold that thought till my next grieving compartment."

If you are speaking to someone, do not mention the decedent or how you are feeling about the loss until your scheduled grieving talk with that person. If the subject comes up during a conversation, then change the subject by saying "We'll talk about that later."

Hopefully you will find the pain of your loss to lessen over time, in frequency and/or intensity.

It isn't so much that time heals; it is more that you learn to heal yourself over time.

Glossary

ADMINISTRATION The *administration* of a Probate Estate is the management and settlement of the decedent's affairs. There are different types of administration. See *Ancillary Administration and Summary administration.*

AFFIANT   An *affiant* is someone who signs an affidavit and swears that it is true in the presence of a Notary Public or other person with authority to administer an oath.

AFFIDAVIT   An *affidavit* is a written statement of fact made by someone voluntarily and under oath, in the presence of a notary public or someone else who has authority to administer an oath.

AGENT   An *agent* is someone who is authorized by another (the principal) to act for or in place of the principal.

ANATOMICAL GIFT   An *anatomical gift* is the donation of all or part of the body of the decedent for a specified purpose, such as transplantation or research.

ANCILLARY ADMINISTRATION An *ancillary administration* is a probate procedure that aids or assists the original (primary) probate proceeding. Ancillary administration is conducted in another state to determine the beneficiary of the decedent's property located within that state, and to determine whether the property is taxable in that state.

ANNUITANT   An *annuitant* is someone who is entitled to receive payments under an annuity contract.

ANNUITY An   *annuity* is a contract that gives someone (the annuitant) the right to receive periodic payments (monthly, quarterly) either for life or for a number of years.

ASCENDANT An *ascendant* of the decedent is his lineal ancestor, i.e.,his parent, grandparent, great-grandparent, etc.

ASSET An *asset* is anything owned by someone that has a value, including personal property (jewelry, paintings, securities, cash, motor vehicles, etc.) and real property (condominiums, vacant lots, acreage, residences, etc.)

ATTESTING WITNESS: An *attesting witness* to a Will is someone who signs the Will, at the request of the person making the Will, in the presence of the person making the Will, for the purpose of proving that the Will maker signed the Will and did so of his own free will.

BENEFICIARY A *beneficiary* is one who benefits from the acts of another person. In this book, we refer to a beneficiary as someone who inherits assets from the decedent.

BOND A *bond*, as used in this book, is a bond in which an insurance company agrees to pay the beneficiaries of the estate for a loss suffered because the Personal Representative failed to do his job properly.

CAVEAT *Caveat* is Latin for "Let him beware." It is a warning for the reader to be careful.

CLAIM A *claim* against the decedent's estate is a demand for payment of a debt of the decedent. To be effective, the claim must be filed with the Probate court within the time limits set by law.

CODICIL A *codicil* to a Will is a supplement or an addition to a Will that changes certain parts of the Will.

COLUMBARIUM A *columbarium* is a vault with niches (spaces) for urns that contain the ashes of cremated bodies.

COMMISSION   As used in this book, a *commission* is compensation that is paid to the Personal Representative for the faithful discharge of his duties.

COMMON LAW MARRIAGE A *common law marriage* is one that is entered into without a state marriage license nor any kind of official marriage ceremony. A common law marriage is created by an agreement to marry, followed by the two living together as man and wife. Most states do not recognize a common law marriage as being a valid marriage.

CREMAINS The word *cremains* is an abbreviation of the term *cremated remains*. It is also referred to as the *ashes* of a person who has been cremated.

DEAD MAN'S STATUTE The *Dead Man's Statute* is a law that prohibits a witness from testifying that the decedent said something in support of a claim against the decedent's estate. For example, if a person owed the decedent money, then that person cannot offer testimony that the decedent wanted to forgive the loan.

DECEDENT The *decedent* is the person who died.

DISSENT To *dissent* is to disagree or object to something. In this book, to dissent from the Will, means that the spouse objects to the amount given in the Will and elects to take the share allowed by law.

DISTRIBUTION The *distribution* of a trust estate or of a Probate Estate is the giving to the beneficiary that part of the estate to which the beneficiary is entitled.

DISBURSE To *disburse* the Probate estate is to use probate funds to pay monies owed by the decedent or by the decedent's estate.

ENCUMBRANCE   An *encumbrance* is a charge or lien against a parcel of real property that reduces the value of the property; for example, mortgages and mechanic's liens are encumbrances.

ESCHEAT   *Escheat* is the right of the state to property that has been abandoned, or property that is unclaimed by any rightful owner.

ESTATE   A person's *Estate* is all of the property (both real and personal property) owned by that person. The decedent's estate may also be referred to as his *Taxable Estate* because all of the decedent's assets must be included when determining whether any Estate taxes are due after the person dies. Compare to *Probate Estate*.

FIDUCIARY   A *fiduciary* is one who holds property in trust for another or one who acts for the benefit of another.

GRANTEE   The *grantee* of a deed (also called the party of the second part) named in a deed is the person who receives title to the property from the grantor.

GRANTOR   A *grantor* is someone who transfers property. The grantor of a deed, (also called the party of the first part), is the person who transfers property to a new owner (the *grantee*). The grantor of a trust is someone who creates the trust and then transfers property into the trust. Also see *settlor*.

HEALTH CARE AGENT   A *Health Care Agent* is someone who is appointed under a Health Care Power of Attorney to make medical decisions for another (the *Principal*) in the event that the Principal is too ill to make those decisions for himself.

HEALTH CARE POWER OF ATTORNEY A *Health Care Power of Attorney* is a written document in which someone (the *Principal*) appoints another (his *Health Care Agent*) to make health care decisions on behalf of the Principal in the event that the Principal is too sick to make such decisions.

HEIR   The state of North Carolina defines the word *heir* as it may appear in a Will or a deed to be synonymous with the word *children*. For example, "... to William Smith and his heirs..." is the same as saying "... to William Smith and his children..." (NCGS 41-6). If the decedent did not have a Will then *heir* means anyone who inherits the property according to the North Carolina Laws of Intestate Succession (NCGS 28A1-1).

HOMESTEAD   The *homestead* is the dwelling that is owned, and occupied as the owner's principal residence.

INDIGENT   A person who is *indigent* is one who is poor, and without funds.

INTESTATE   *Intestate* means not having a Will or dying without a Will. *Testate* is to have a Will or dying with a Will.

IRREVOCABLE CONTRACT   An *irrevocable* contract is a contract that cannot be revoked, withdrawn, or cancelled by any of the parties to that contract.

KEY MAN INSURANCE   *Key man insurance* is an insurance policy designed to protect a company from economic loss in the event that an important employee of the company becomes disabled or dies.

LEGALESE   *Legalese* refers to the use of legal terms and confusing text that is used by many attorneys to draft legal documents.

LETTERS OF ADMINISTRATION   *Letters of Administration* is a document, issued by the Probate court, giving the person who is appointed as Administrator, authority to take possession of and to administer the estate of the decedent.

LETTERS TESTAMENTARY   *Letters Testamentary* is a document given to the person who is the Executor of the decedent's Will that gives the Executor authority to take possession of and to administer the estate of the decedent.

LIEN   A *lien* is a charge or a claim on someone's property as security for a debt. If the debt is not paid, the lender can take legal action to get possession of the property as payment for the debt.

LIFE ESTATE   A *life estate* interest in real property is the right to possess and occupy that property for so long as the holder of the life estate lives.

JURISDICTION   A *jurisdiction* is a territorial range of authority or the legal power to hear cases. For example, in North Carolina, the Superior Court has jurisdiction for probate matters.

LINEAL DESCENDANT   A *lineal descendant* of the decedent is someone from a later generation, such as the decedent's child, grandchild, great-grandchild. The North Carolina Law of Intestate Succession includes adopted children as descendants of the decedent.

LITIGATION   *Litigation* is the process of carrying on a lawsuit, i.e., to sue for some right or remedy in a court of law.

LIVING WILL   A *Living Will* is a Health Care Directive that gives instructions about whether life support systems should be withheld in the event that the person who signs the Living Will is terminally ill or in a persistent vegetative state and unable to speak for himself.

MEDICAID *Medicaid* is a public assistance program sponsored jointly by the federal and state government to provide medical care for people with low income.

NET PROCEEDS The *net proceeds* of a sale is the sale price less costs and expenses paid to make the sale.

NET WORTH A person's *net worth* is the value of all of the property that he owns less the monies he owes.

NEXT OF KIN *Next of kin* has two meanings in law: *next of kin* can refer to a person's nearest blood relation or it can refer to those people (not necessarily blood relations) who are entitled to inherit the property of the decedent if the decedent died without a will.

PERJURY *Perjury* is lying under oath. The false statement can be made as a witness in court or by signing an Affidavit. Perjury is a criminal offense.

PERSONAL PROPERTY *Personal property* is all property owned by a person that is not real property (real estate). It includes cars, stocks, house furnishings, jewelry, etc. Personal property is sometimes called ***personalty***.

PERSONAL REPRESENTATIVE The *Personal Representative* is someone (the Administrator or Executor) appointed by the Probate court to settle the decedent's estate and to distribute whatever is left to the proper beneficiary.

PER STIRPES GIFT A *per stirpes* gift is a gift which is given to a group of people such that if one of them dies before the gift is made, then that deceased person's share goes to his/her lineal descendants.

POWER OF ATTORNEY A *Power of Attorney* is a document in which the person who signs the document (the *Principal*) gives another person (his *Agent*) authority to do certain things on behalf of the Principal.

PRE-NUPTIAL AGREEMENT A *pre-nuptial agreement* (also known as an *antenuptial agreement*) is an agreement made prior to marriage whereby a couple determines how their property is to be managed during their marriage and how their property is to be divided should one die, or they later divorce.

PROBATE *Probate* is a court procedure in which a court determines the existence of a valid Will and then supervises the distribution of the Probate Estate of the decedent.

PROBATE ESTATE The *Probate Estate* is that part of the decedent's estate that is subject to probate. It includes property that the decedent owned in his name only. It does not include property that was jointly with rights of survivorship, nor property held "in trust for" or "for the benefit of" someone.

RECEIVER A *Receiver* is a person appointed by the court to preserve property when there is a pending court procedure and there is danger that the property may be lost, removed or injured, before the matter is resolved.

REAL PROPERTY *Real property,* also known as *real estate,* is land and anything permanently attached to the land such as buildings and fences.

REGISTERED AGENT A *Registered Agent* of a corporation is someone who is authorized to act on behalf of the company and accept service of process in the event the company is sued.

REPARATION   *Reparation* is money paid to make up for an injury or wrongdoing.

RESIDUARY BENEFICIARY   A *residuary beneficiary* is a beneficiary named in a Will who is to receive all or part of whatever is left of the Probate Estate once all gifts specified in the Will are made and after the decedent's bills, taxes and costs of probate have been paid.

RESIDUARY ESTATE   A *residuary estate* is that part of a probate estate that is left after all expenses and costs of administration have been paid and specific gifts have been distributed.

SETTLOR   A *settlor* is someone who furnishes property that is placed in a trust. If the settlor is also the creator of the trust, then the settlor is also referred to as the Grantor.

SPENDTHRIFT TRUST   A *Spendthrift Trust* is a trust created to provide monies to a beneficiary, and at the same time protect the beneficiary from the monies from being taken by the his creditors.

STATUTE OF LIMITATION   A *statute of limitation* is a federal or state law that sets maximum time periods for taking legal action. Once the time set out in the statute passes, no legal action can be taken.

SUMMARY ADMINISTRATION   *Summary Administration* is a short, relatively simple probate procedure designed to settle small estates.

TENANCY BY THE ENTIRETY   A *Tenancy by the Entirety* is the name of real property that is held by husband and wife. It has the same legal effect as a Joint Tenancy with right of survivorship.

TENANCY IN COMMON   *Tenancy in common* is a form of ownership such that each tenant owns his/her share without any claim to that share by the other tenants. There is no right of survivorship. Once a tenant in common dies, his/her share belongs to the tenant's estate and not to the remaining owners of the property.

TESTATE   *Testate* means having a Will or dying with a Will.

TITLE INSURANCE   *Title Insurance* is a policy issued by a title company after searching title to the property. The policy insures the accuracy of the title search against a claim of a defective title.

TRUST AGREEMENT A *trust agreement* is document in which someone (the Grantor or Settlor) creates a trust and appoints a trustee to manage property placed into the trust. The usual purpose of the trust is to benefit persons or charities named by the Grantor as beneficiaries of the trust.

TRUSTEE   A *trustee* is a person, or institution, who accepts the duty of caring for property for the benefit of another.

UNDUE INFLUENCE   *Undue influence* is pressure, influence or persuasion that overpowers a person's free will or judgment, so that a person acts according to the will or purpose of the dominating party.

WAIVER   A *waiver* is the intentional and voluntary giving up of a known right.

WARRANTY DEED   A *warranty deed* is a deed in which someone (the Grantor) transfers the property to another (the Grantee) and guarantees good title i.e., the Grantor guarantees that he has the right to transfer the property, and that no one else has any right to the property.

INDEX

A

B

141 North Carolina Statutes are referenced in
Guiding Those Left Behind In North Carolina

Each state has its own set of laws relating to the settlement of a person's estate. The North Carolina laws that are referenced in this book are very different from the laws of other states. The author is in now in the process of "translating" *Guiding Those Left Behind . . .* for the rest of the states; that is, to write a book that incorporates the laws of the state into a book that describes how to settle the affairs of a decedent in that state, and how to prepare an estate plan that is appropriate for the state.

Arizona, California, Florida, Illinois, North Carolina, New Jersey, New York, Ohio, Pennsylvania and Texas are now in print. The following books are scheduled for release by January, 2001:

Guiding Those Left Behind In Massachusetts
Guiding Those Left Behind In Michigan
Guiding Those Left Behind In Georgia

The following books are scheduled for release by April 2001:

Guiding Those Left Behind in Indiana
Guiding Those Left Behind In Maryland
Guiding Those Left Behind In Virginia
Guiding Those Left Behind in Washington

To order a book call (800) 824-0823.
Visit our Web site   http://www.eaglepublishing.com to check whether books from other states are available at this time.